SO-DGK-946

Representing the Immigrant Experience

Judaic Traditions in Literature, Music, and Art
Ken Frieden and Harold Bloom, Series Editors

מאָררים ראָזענפעלד.

Morris Rosenfeld. From Lider bukh, ershter teyl
(Book of Poems, Part One) (New York: Grover Bros., 1897).

Representing the Immigrant Experience

Morris Rosenfeld
and the Emergence
of Yiddish Literature
in America

M A R C   M I L L E R

Syracuse University Press

Copyright © 2007 by Syracuse University Press
Syracuse, New York 13244–5160
All Rights Reserved

First Edition 2007
07   08   09   10   11   12   6   5   4   3   2   1

The paper used in this publication meets the minimum requirements of
American National Standard for Information Sciences—Permanence of
Paper for Printed Library Materials, ANSI Z39.48–1984.∞™

For a listing of books published and distributed by Syracuse University Press,
visit our Web site at SyracuseUniversityPress.syr.edu.

ISBN-13: 978-0-8156-3110-1 (cloth)   ISBN-10: 0-8156-3110-3 (cloth)
ISBN-13: 978-0-8156-3136-1 (pbk.)   ISBN-10: 0-8156-3136-7 (pbk.)

Library of Congress Cataloging-in-Publication Data
Miller, Marc.
Representing the immigrant experience : Morris Rosenfeld and the emergence
of Yiddish literature in America / Marc Miller.—1st ed.
p. cm.—(Judaic traditions in literature, music, and art)
Includes bibliographical references and index.
ISBN 0–8156–3110–3 (hardcover : alk. paper)—
ISBN 0–8156–3136–7 (pbk. : alk. paper)
1. Rosenfeld, Morris, 1862–1923. 2. Poets, Yiddish—Biography. 3. Yiddish
literature—United States—History and criticism. I. Title.
PJ5129.R6Z78 2007
839'.113—dc22   2006033605

Manufactured in the United States of America

For my teachers Eugene Orenstein and Dan Miron

"Sweat Shop." Watercolor by Therese Weinberger. Courtesy of the artist.

MARC MILLER is assistant professor of Yiddish language, literature, and culture at Emory University, where he holds a joint appointment in the Department of German Studies and the Institute for Jewish Studies. He has published essays in *East European Jewish Affairs, Hebrew Linguistics, Journal of Modern Jewish Studies,* and *Monatshefte für deutschsprachige Literatur und Kultur.* He is currently at work on a book-length study of the Holocaust novel in English, French, German, Hebrew, and Yiddish.

Contents

Preface

Before Isaac Bashevis Singer presented the life of the Eastern European Jewish immigrant to a large, international audience, several earlier Yiddish writers filled this role, translating their works into many of the world's languages. Popular authors such as Sholem Aleykhem (1859–1916) and Sholem Asch (1880–1957) gained multilingual fame in the early decades of the twentieth century with short stories and novels that represented a world foreign to many Jewish and non-Jewish readers alike. But the first Yiddish writer to serve successfully as an interpreter and representative of this world was Morris Rosenfeld (1862–1923).

Rosenfeld immigrated to America from his native Russia in 1886, and began his long literary career. Composing poems initially to agitate his working-class readership into social protest, Rosenfeld published his work in the early American Yiddish press. Periodicals such as *Der arbeter tsaytung* (The Workers' Newspaper), *Der folksadvokat* (The People's Advocate), *Di varheyt* (The Truth), and *Forverts* (Forward) were politically tendentious newspapers that promoted ideologies such as socialism, communism, and anarchism. The poetry that Rosenfeld published in these and other, similar publications in the 1880s and 1890s adhered to the strict tenets of the "Sweatshop" poem, a genre he helped create in modern Yiddish literature.

Rosenfeld's early works were similar in tone, structure, and motif to those of his cohorts, most notably Yoysef Bovshover (1873–1915), Dovid Edelshtat (1866–1892), and Morris Vinchevsky (1856–1932). In the pages of the radical press, these poets—and scores more—called on their working-class readers to rise up against their bosses and bring an end to the capitalist system. Like the nineteenth-century poetry of the *haskala* (Jewish Enlightenment) that preceded it, Sweatshop poetry was didactic and its raison d'être was wholly pragmatic. Unlike the *haskala* poets, however, who often called on their readers to embrace secular, European culture, Rosenfeld, Vinchevsky, Bovshover, and Edelshtat demanded complete social revolution.

Although Rosenfeld began his career in this vein—with almost no Yiddish literary tradition to draw upon—he soon moved beyond the narrow, propagandistic parameters of his early work to produce some of the most lasting poetry in the Yiddish language. He abandoned his calls to arms and shifted the focus of his poetry to the immigrant self. Instead of imploring workers to revolt against the upper classes, Rosenfeld began to lament the sad life of the immigrant worker who toiled and lived under brutal conditions. This new focus resulted in the reification of the sweatshop as a metaphor for the existence of the individual.

In works such as "Di svet shap" (The Sweatshop), "Fartsveyflung" (Despair), and "Der trern miliyoner" (The Teardrop Millionaire), which the literary scholar Leo Wiener collected, translated, and published in 1898 as *Songs from the Ghetto*, Rosenfeld imbued the shop with deep strains of literary sentimentalism and melodrama, delivering a highly emotional impact to his growing readership. In these works, which I consider his "mature" Sweatshop poems, Rosenfeld developed a poetics of pessimism and depression. His voice is the sad voice of the immigrant worker who bemoans his existential condition, trapped until death in a life of poverty, labor, and sadness. The great achievement of Rosenfeld's poetry lies in mirroring the immigrant experience and the literary capabilities of his audience by addressing the everyday life of the average shop worker. Rosenfeld's poetic speakers and protagonists hate their jobs, long for rest, and spend little time with their families.

Rosenfeld offered his readers a plot they could understand, a highly emotional, melodramatic narrative with which they could connect. He was the ghetto poet whose own life experiences as a sweatshop worker played a key role in validating his poetic expression. Indeed, for many of his Yiddish critics, Rosenfeld's poetry was an authentic expression of the Eastern European immigrant. As a wide cross section of readers responded to this unique, poetic approach, *Songs from the Ghetto* was not only reprinted a number of times over the next decade, but also translated into a host of European languages, making Morris Rosenfeld the first guide to and interpreter of Eastern European Jewish culture for a foreign audience.

Despite the success of his work in his lifetime, however, Rosenfeld does not have a secure place in the canon of modern Yiddish literature. With the emergence of the group of American poets known as "Di yunge" (The Young Ones) during the second decade of the twentieth century, modernist aesthetics came to dominate criticism of Yiddish poetry. These poets derided Rosenfeld as an old-fashioned, politically tendentious poet who produced little more than rhymed propaganda for the Yiddish press. As this view of the poet became ensconced in the Yiddish critical establishment, poetic anthologies and studies increasingly limited their representation of Rosenfeld's work.

Yet Rosenfeld deserves a careful literary reassessment free of ideological filters, whether Yiddishist or modernist. Two current circumstances open the door to such a reassessment: the critical abandonment of the idea of a formal canon, especially problematic in Yiddish absent any consensus, and the current blurring of the distinction between low and high cultures. Although Rosenfeld's place in a putative canon of Yiddish literature is uncertain, his role in the development of Yiddish literature is unquestionable. The current volume represents the first full-length study to treat Rosenfeld from a literary rather than a political or ideological perspective.

Acknowledgments

I would like to begin by thanking the people in my current (and hopefully longtime) home, Emory University. At Emory, I am fortunate to have two academic homes, one in Jewish studies and the other in German. In the Department of Jewish Studies, I would like to thank Michael Berger, David Blumenthal, Michael Broyde, Bill Gilders, Hazel Gold, Eric Goldstein, Benny Hari, Jeffrey Lesser, Deborah Lipstadt, Gordon Newby, Marina Rustow, Don Seeman, Joseph Skibell, Ken Stein, and Ofra Yeglin. My thanks also to the staff members of the Rabbi Donald A. Tam Institute for Jewish Studies: Mary Jo Duncanson, Adenike Brewington, and Malory Mibab. In the Department of German Studies, I would like to thank Max Aue, Erik Butler, Peter Höyng, Marianne Lancaster, Jamie Melton, Caroline Schaumann, Erdmann Waniek, and Viola Westbrook, as well as Silke Delamare and Elizabeth Soilis, our administrators. Also, I would like to thank the Jewish Studies Enrichment Fund of Emory University for supporting the indexing of this book.

I would like to thank Ellen Goodman of Syracuse University Press, who acquired my manuscript, as well as Ken Frieden, coeditor of the Judaic Traditions in Literature, Music, and Art series. I would also like to thank Nick Fabian for his editorial assistance.

Representing the Immigrant Experience is based on the dissertation I completed at Columbia University, and is the culmination of many years of education. I was fortunate to have earned both my bachelor's and my master's degrees in the Jewish Studies Department of McGill University, where I was first exposed to the language, literature, and culture of Eastern European Jews. To Esther Frank, my first Yiddish teacher: Thank you for setting me on my path, and for introducing me to the writings of Sholem Asch, H. D. Nomberg, and the ever-disturbing Lamed Shapiro. To Professor Gershon Hundert: Thank you for guiding me through the world of Polish Jewish history and for your rigorous demands. I apologize for sometimes not being completely alert in your eight A.M. classes. Professor Ruth Wisse: Thank you for your classes in modern Jewish literature and for the time you spent in your office answering the questions of an undergraduate fan. In the preface to your endnotes in *A Little Love in Big Manhattan,* you write that your focus was narrow but that you left tracks for future scholars to pursue. I picked up one of those tracks and the product is now before you.

There are two anecdotes I delight in relating about Professor Eugene Orenstein. In the first, after handing him my completed final examination for his course on Zionism in my first semester at McGill, I turned to leave the silent classroom. Professor Orenstein glanced at the first page of my exam booklet and observed, in a voice well above a whisper before the rest of the test-taking students: "Mr. Miller, I am not an expert on hieroglyphics." In the second, while lecturing on the literary representation of the Eastern European town, Professor Orenstein asked whether anyone would like to comment about I. M. Weissenberg's novella *A shtetl.* Being a budding expert trying to impress my favorite professor, I raised my hand and said, confidently: "It is unlike anything I've ever read in Yiddish literature," to which Professor Orenstein quipped, "Well, obviously you haven't read very much."

In the course of my six years at McGill, I took every course Professor Orenstein offered and spent three semesters with him in independent study. Eugene: What can I say? You showed me the way. When, at the age of twenty-three, I told you I wanted to write a book about Mendele-Moykher Sforim and Sholem Aleykhem, you told me Dan Miron had already done so and introduced me to one of my favorite books, *A Traveler Disguised*. In terms of Yiddish literature, you introduced me to Yoysef Opatoshu (I am especially grateful for "Moris un zayn zun Philip"), H. Leyvik, Y. Y. Shvarts, Y. Y. Siegel, and many other writers, too numerous to list here. Your ambitious expectations challenged me. You sent me to the library on countless occasions to absorb the books—including, in my freshman year, Solomon Maimon's autobiography—you expected me to have already read.

At the YIVO *zumer* program, I was fortunate to have sharpened my Yiddish skills with the help of some excellent teachers. Thanks to Professor Ellen Kellman and Dr. Mordkhe Shekhter who helped me to advance my linguistic skills. To Professor Avrom Novershtern: Thank you for broadening my scope of Yiddish literature. Thank you for *Ba nakht afn altn mark* and especially "Zlochev, mayn heym." When you commented that someone ought to write a study of the persona Moyshe Leyb, I followed your suggestion and made it the topic of my master's thesis.

Much of my research was completed at the YIVO Institute for Jewish Research in New York City. My thanks to Zachary Baker, Gunnar Berg, Krysia Fisher, Leo Greenbaum, Chana Mlotek, Fruma Mohrer, Dr. Allan Nadler, Aaron Taub, Marek Web, and Bina Weinreich. And my special thanks to Herbert Lazarus.

I am grateful to my colleagues for their help in all matters. Professor Olga Litvak: As I write these words, you are still a rising star, not yet a full-fledged bigshot. I am confident that you will one day rule the world of Russian Jewish history and I hope, at that point, you will still return my calls. Thank you for helping keep my dissertation honest. Professor Kalman "Keith Ian" Weiser: You constantly amaze me with your intellectual depth and stunning understanding of language. I am going on record to say that you

speak the best Yiddish of our *(apikorsish)* generation. Professor
Philip Abraham Hollander: It is hard for me to express the debt I
owe you, but I will try. You are one of the most creative people I
know. Your understanding of poetry is incredible. Thank you for
sitting with me for hours when you should have been doing your
own work.

I would like to thank the Memorial Foundation for Jewish
Culture, the Atran Foundation, and the Lucius N. Littauer Foundation for their support in the writing and research of the dissertation on which this book is based.

The Department of Germanic Languages and Literatures at
Columbia University is a very special place. Thank you, Professor
Dorothea Von Mücke, Professor Harro Müller, Professor Andreas
Huyssen, Professor Mark Anderson, and Richard Korb, for your
guidance and advice. Thank you, Peggy Quisenberry, for your
warmth, kindness, and for always putting out something sweet in
the office. And thank you, Bill Dellinger, for all of your help, especially for untying bureaucratic knots and guiding me through the
Soviet-like maze of Columbia University.

At Columbia, I was fortunate to have learned from many im-
pressive people. For three semesters at the Jewish Theological
Seminary (JTS), I studied Yiddish literature, *af yidish, vi es geher tsu
zayn,* with Professor David Roskies. *Oy, Reboyne sheloylem, ven ikh
bin Dovid Roskies . . .* Sholem Aleykhem's *melamed* wanted to be
Rothchild, but I always wanted to be David Roskies. Reb Dovid:
One of the first books in this field that I ever read was *Against the
Apocalypse* and it was the first place I learned about the figures of
the *talush* and my role model, the *bal guf.* Although Eugene had
prepared me well, there was still much I didn't know although, at
the time, I didn't know it. Thank you for *Laykhtzin un fremelay,
Sipurei mayses, Der Nister,* and much, much more. Thank you for
letting me come to your office and just shmooze about Yiddish literature and other unrelated topics.

Professor Rakhmiel Peltz: Thank you for accepting me into the doctoral program at Columbia, for your Yiddish courses on ethnography, sociology, and even grammar, and for opening up the world of Soviet Yiddish culture to me. Your interdisciplinary approach has shaped the way I look at Yiddish, and your teaching has helped shape this book.

Miriam Hoffman: *Miriyiml, vos zol ikh zogn?* You're the best. Without you, I would not have known the true wonders of Itsik Manger and Moyshe Nadir. Thank you for your advanced Yiddish classes, for the folk songs, the folk stories, the *shprikhverter* (G-rated as well as *grob*), and all of the other amazing resources in your *shlislekh*. You were a great mentor and it was an honor teaching for you.

My dissertation committee. Professor Jeffrey Shandler: Thank you for your insights and for your mentoring while I taught at Rutgers University. Your comments have helped me to improve both my writing and my teaching skills. Professor Kathryn Hellerstein: *Eyder ikh hob gepisht,* before you could even call me a bona fide *pisher,* before I even knew there was such a thing as a persona, there were your articles and your book on Moyshe-Leyb Halpern. Since then, he has come to mean much to me, and I thank you for being my first guide to his works. Professor Jeremy Dauber: I am grateful for the brief time we spent together at Columbia. Thank you for reading and commenting on chapters of my dissertation, and for your cogent and helpful comments.

Professor Michael Stanislawski: Thank you for your unswerving loyalty and support (which I hope will not run out just because I graduated). Whether it was to read early drafts of my dissertation or to serve as my weekly therapist on issues having nothing or little to do with Yiddish, you were always there for me. During my time at Columbia, you were a solid, grounding force. You helped me to feel secure in an insecure world (at no charge).

Akharon akharon khaviv, Professor Dan Miron: Not only do I feel lucky to be alive at the same time as you; I feel blessed that you were my teacher and adviser. When I was accepted to Columbia, I could hardly believe that I would be studying with the author of *A Traveler Disguised,* "Sholem Aleykhem—Person, Persona, Presence," and *Der imazh fun shtetl.* Your works inspire me in the way they constantly challenge accepted beliefs and question the validity of almost everything. Thanks to you, I look first and foremost to the text for proof. Thank you for allowing me to translate your works into English and for being a part of *The Image of the Shtetl.* That first week of my first graduate seminar on American Yiddish poetry, when you sent us home to read Rosenfeld, I was surprised to learn how many negative biases I had absorbed—biases I now expose in my work. After rereading the poet, I was only too eager to respond to your suggestion that "someone should write a dissertation about Morris Rosenfeld." Like Eugene's, your influence on me has been profound, and it is with profound gratitude that I dedicate my book to you both.

To Terry Weinberger Bohbot: Thank you for giving me life. I really appreciate that. When I first came to Columbia, you bought me a mini refrigerator for my dorm room on the condition that I thank you in the acknowledgments of my first book. Thanks for the fridge, Mom. More important, thank you for your unending support and encouragement. I am not the most talented scholar in the world, but your praise has always guided me through periods of despair and frustration.

To Pamela Beth Brill, my wife: You keep me real in an unreal world and I love you. Finally, to our little man-cub, Ezra Elijah: Thank you for giving me joy every single day.

Representing the Immigrant Experience

1

The First Yiddish Best Seller

In 1897, a year that marked a crucial turning point in his career, the poet Morris Rosenfeld composed a four-page letter entitled "Mayn lebns geshikhte in kurtsn" (My Life Story in Brief) to Harvard professor Leo Wiener. This letter now serves as an introduction to Rosenfeld's collected correspondence and as the primary source of information about his early life.[1] Wiener—whose short-lived, yet intense interest in Yiddish literature led him to write, among other important studies, a pioneering history of this field[2]—played a decisive role in the career of the poet. In 1898, Wiener published the first translation of Rosenfeld's poetry: *Songs from the Ghetto* would serve as the basic text for the transmission of Rosenfeld's work into a host of continental European languages and would spark his decade-long international fame. The poet clearly understood the potential significance of Wiener's interest in his work and therefore cultivated his connection with the prominent scholar. In response to the professor's request for autobiographical details, Rosenfeld sent him "My Life Story in Brief," which Wiener used as the basis for his biographical remarks on Rosenfeld in the preface to *Songs from the Ghetto*.[3] Although somewhat self-serving, this document nonetheless represents the sole record of the poet's early life.[4]

Morris Rosenfeld was born in 1862 in Boksha, a village in the Suvalk province of Russian Poland where his two grandfathers were fishermen. Rosenfeld's father, who also worked as a fisherman, supplemented his income as a military tailor, carrying out lucrative contract work for the Russian army. At the age of ten, Rosenfeld moved with his family to Warsaw, where they remained for four years. In 1876, the family returned to Boksha, where twelve of their fourteen children died during a cholera epidemic; only Morris and his youngest brother, Joseph, survived. Up until his thirteenth year, Rosenfeld attended *kheyder* (traditional primary Jewish school). From fourteen to eighteen, Rosenfeld spent most of his time studying traditional Jewish texts in the *beys medresh* (study house) or learning to sew in his father's workshop, a skill that would play a significant role in his later life and poetic work. At eighteen, Rosenfeld was married "to my mother's cousin, a very rich but very ugly girl with whom I lived for six months and then divorced."[5] A year later, he married Asne-Beyle Yevarkovski, who would remain his lifelong companion.

In 1882, Rosenfeld left Suvalk province and, like an increasing number of Eastern European Jews at this time, traveled to America, where he remained for six months. Unable to find sustained or satisfactory employment in New York, Rosenfeld returned home, only to leave again less than a year later, for Amsterdam, in the hope of establishing a trade as a diamond polisher and sending for his family. It was not to be. After six months, he quit Holland and returned to Russia.

In early 1883, Rosenfeld again fled the Russian empire, this time to avoid the military draft. He found work in England as a sweatshop sewing machine operator, a job he would perform for the next fifteen years. Working and living in London's East End, Rosenfeld got his first taste of the intense urban poverty and squalor he and his family would suffer throughout the following two decades. After several months, Rosenfeld's wife, Asne-Beyle, and their newborn daughter, Dora, joined him in England. There the family struggled to survive oppressive economic conditions that were only exacerbated by the death of the couple's newborn twins, Abraham and Lilly.

In the middle of 1886, the Rosenfeld family left London for the United States. Like many other Eastern European Jewish immigrants, they settled on New York's Lower East Side, which would become the background for the poet's literary works. Asne-Beyle gave birth to three more children in America: Joseph, Frieda-Iona, and Rose. She supplemented her husband's meager sweatshop income through the sale of wigs she made at home. On several occasions, Rosenfeld was forced to seek employment in other parts of the city. Thus, for a short period in 1892, he lived and worked in Brooklyn while his wife and children remained in Yonkers, just north of New York and, before the development of effective public transport, not a reasonable daily commute.[6]

Although Rosenfeld worked long hours, he did not neglect his literary aspirations. He began his career almost as soon as he arrived in the United States, publishing his early works in this country's infant Yiddish press, which would play a formative role in the development of Yiddish literature in America. The first American Yiddish newspapers were short-lived enterprises; virtually no copies have survived.[7] Published irregularly, most were no more than a few pages long and contained news articles chiefly about current events in Europe. For example, *Di post* (The Post), considered the very first Yiddish newspaper in America, was founded exclusively to provide Yiddish readers with information about the Franco-Prussian War.[8] This early preoccupation with news of European events over and above news of local events persisted through the 1880s, leading the literary critic Sh. Niger (Tsharni) to characterize this period of the Yiddish press in the United States as "more old-country than American."[9]

The development of the Yiddish press in the United States began in earnest during the 1880s, when the mass immigration of Eastern European Jews provided a Yiddish readership large enough to sustain a number of Yiddish newspapers, many of which actually flourished. The first significant Yiddish newspaper—and one of the first Yiddish socialist newspapers in America—was the weekly *Di naye tsayt* (The New Era), although it survived for only four editions. *Di naye tsayt* was also the first project of Abraham Cahan, a pioneer in the American Yiddish press, who would go on to edit such important socialist newspapers as *Der arbeter tsaytung* (Workers' Newspaper) and *Forverts* (Forward). Another important early Yiddish publication was *Di nyu yorker yidishe folkstsaytung* (The New York Jewish People's Newspaper). Founded by two Jewish factory workers who came to New York from Massachusetts with their savings, this weekly had as its expressed purpose the education of the Jewish proletariat. While addressing the "worker question," it also highlighted specific moments in Jewish history.[10] M. Y. Mints, one of the two coeditors, was a self-professed "Hovev-Zion" (Lover of Zion) and an active supporter of Jewish settlement in the Land of Israel.[11] Thus the newspaper, although specifically left-wing in outlook, sometimes published articles that were proto-Zionist. At a time when political lines between Zionists and socialists were still sharply drawn, left-wing organizations often accused *Di nyu yorker yidishe folkstsaytung* of "treacherous nationalism and Jewish chauvinism."[12]

Rosenfeld made his literary debut in *Di nyu yorker yidishe folkstsaytung* on December 17, 1886, with "Dos yor 1886" (The Year 1886). His first poem consists of thirteen eight-line stanzas written in the style of high bombast and common sentiment characteristic of a popular nineteenth-century genre of Hebrew and Yiddish poetry in which poets examined the previous year on the cusp of a new one.[13] It adheres to the nineteenth-century *haskala* mode of poetic expression, which called on Jewish readers to abandon traditional ways of life and embrace, among other values, secular, European culture and education. In Rosenfeld's long, raw poem, the poetic speaker addresses the Jewish people, demanding that they awake from their passive stupor. This call is a familiar one, reminiscent of "Hakitsah ami" (Awake My People), the famous 1863 work by the leading poet of the Hebrew *haskala*, Yehuda Leyb Gordon (known commonly by his acronym "Yalag"):

Hakitsah ami ad matai tishana
en gaz halayl hashemesh he'ira
hakitsah sim eynkha aneh ve'ana
uzemankha umekomkha ana hakira.

[Awake, my people! How long will you sleep?
The night has passed, the sun shines through.
Awake, cast your eyes hither and yon
Recognize your time and your place.][14]

Mikhl Gordon, Yalag's brother-in-law, would adapt this motif to Yiddish poetry. In his poem also entitled "Awake My People," the Yiddish poet of the *haskala* in fact quotes the first stanza of Yalag's poem in an epigraph.[15]

The speaker in "The Year 1886" urges the Jewish people to free themselves of the shackles imposed on them by organized religion:

Zisnke lidelekh zingt men dir ayn,
in vig "fanatizmus"—shlofstu geshmak.
Men zogt dir, az andersh ken gor nit zayn
ze nor, mayn folk, vi men firt dikh in zak.
Dayonim—rabonim—shvindler der velt!
Zey shpiln farshtelt zeyer role atsind,
zey lozn dikh iber shreklekh gekvelt
un redn dir ayn, az du laydst far dayn zind.[16]

[Sweet songs are sung to you,
in the cradle of "fanaticism"—you sleep soundly.
You are told that it can be no other way

just see, my people, how you are being trapped.
Judges [traditional judges of religious courts]—rabbis—swindlers
   of the world!
They mask themselves as they play their roles,
they leave you terribly tortured
and convince you that you are suffering because of your sins.]

Like his *haskala* predecessors, Rosenfeld lashes out against the traditional authority figures of the Jewish community. Although these religious functionaries held great power among Jews in the old country, their influence and significance diminished in America. Aware of this power shift, Rosenfeld would prove instrumental in redirecting the momentum of the *haskala* tradition toward a new enemy.

Two weeks after his debut, Rosenfeld published his second poem, "Far der nyu yorker yidishe folkstsaytung" (For the New York Jewish People's Newspaper). In it, the speaker singles out the bosses of industry as the new enemy of the Jewish working class. This is Rosenfeld's first Sweatshop poem, a genre he would experiment with and develop throughout his career. His early efforts in this genre—like those of his contemporaries—are calls to arms in which the poetic speaker attempts to rouse a working-class readership to revolt against the upper classes. These poems almost always end on an optimistic note, predicting the success of the workers' efforts; they are similar in theme and tone to the poems of Morris Vinchevsky, who began writing Yiddish poetry in 1884, and of Dovid Edelshtat and Yoysef Bovshover, who wrote chiefly in the 1890s. Most critics classify Rosenfeld, Vinchevsky, Edelshtat, and Bovshover—the main representatives of their literary generation—as the "Sweatshop" poets of Yiddish literature.

In 1888, Rosenfeld issued his first collection of poetry, *Di gloke* (The Bell),[17] an allusion to the influential poem by Friedrich Schiller "Das Lied von der Glocke" (The Song of the Bell).[18] Yankev

Merison, a friend who helped lay out the proofs for the collection, tells how a butcher cousin of Rosenfeld guaranteed the sales of the book with its printer. Although a few thousand copies were published, Merison writes, only about twenty were sold; the rest were bought by the butcher, whose "mice fed on their remains."[19] In a later introductory note composed for a German collection of his poetry, Rosenfeld writes that he was so dissatisfied with *Di gloke*, which was a critical as well as financial failure, that he bought up and destroyed many copies of the book himself.[20]

Several of the poems in *Di gloke* first appeared in *Di nyu yorker yidishe folkstsaytung*[21] and in *Arbeter fraynd* (Worker's Friend), a socialist-anarchist newspaper founded in 1885 in London and edited by Philip Krantz.[22] These poems—most notably, "Vi lang nokh?" (How Much Longer?), "Biz danen!" (Until Here!), "Di alte sisteme" (The Old System), "Di revolutsiyon" (The Revolution), and "Di tsukunft" (The Future)—develop the central theme of Rosenfeld's early poetry, the injustice of a capitalist system in which workers die for the profit of their rich bosses. Like the earlier works, almost all of these poems have optimistic endings in which the speaker asserts that the day is near when the old system will be destroyed by the successful workers' revolution.

One of the most important values in Rosenfeld's Sweatshop and other early works is truth. Repeatedly, the speakers of Rosenfeld's poems, many of whom address the workers in a similar voice, insist on uncovering the real mechanisms of the capitalist world. And repeatedly, they refer to the owners as "royber" (robbers), "merder" (murderers), and "shvindler" (swindlers), insisting that the rich have achieved and maintain their status through immoral means. Often, the dead appear to the living protagonists—usually within the context of a dream—and enlighten them with the truth. In Jewish tradition, when a person dies, he or she enters *oylem ha'emes* (the true world). Rosenfeld plays on this idea, as did several nineteenth-century Hebrew and Yiddish writers. In this mode, the dead are temporarily rejuvenated that they may convey their crucial, privileged knowledge to the protagonists, endowing them with "true" knowledge known only to them. This motif appears in Rosenfeld's early, phantasmagorical poem "Der troym af bruklin brik" (The Dream on the Brooklyn Bridge). Its speaker relates how one evening, while strolling along the walkway of the newly constructed Brooklyn Bridge, he stops to rest on a bench and quickly dozes off. Suddenly, he feels the bridge begin to swing and rock, he sees flames flare up, and he hears the strains of a choir of unseen voices emerge from below:

Blut un trern gor on mosn,
zaynen do gevorn fargosn,
dos kenen mir aleyn nit shpirn
un arbetendik shver, vifl hobn farlorn
do zeyere yunge yorn,
mentshn, kent ir do nokh shpatsirn![23]

[An unlimited amount of blood and tears,
flowed here,
so many that we cannot breathe
and working hard, how many lost
their youth here,
people, you are still able to stroll here!]

The poem's protagonist quickly realizes that these are the voices of the workers who died during the building of the bridge. The construction of the bridge, which was completed in 1886—two years before the poem was published—reportedly claimed the lives of twenty-seven workers. As he would do throughout his career, most notably, within the context of the Eastern European Jewish immigrant experience, Rosenfeld poeticized historical and social reality. The speaker of the poem pleads with the East River to spit out the "heroes" it has swallowed. After a moment of ominous and suspenseful silence, a row of skeletons emerges from the water and lines up along the bridge to perform a dance macabre. The dead laborers deliver the following message for the protagonist to convey to the living, working masses:

> Brider, ir velkhe nokh laydt,
> vemens fleysh men shindt un men shnaydt—
> a bayshpil fun undz nemt aykh arop!
> Lakht oys "yene velt," nit gloybt in shpeter,
> tsuflikt tsurayst di brutale bleter
> velkhe dreyen aykh durkh gloybn dem kop!
>
> Vakht uf brider mit mut!
> Rakhe nemt far undzer blut!—
> Tsolt di merder di banditn
> vi zey hobn rekht fardint.
> Ramt zey oys fun ayer mitn
> an ende tsu knekhtshaft makht geshvind![24]
>
> [Brothers, you who still suffer,
> whose flesh is flayed and cut—
> learn from our example!
> Forget about "the world to come," don't believe in later,
> pluck and tear out the brutal pages
> which mix up your minds with beliefs!
>
> Arise with courage brothers!
> Take revenge for our blood!—
> Pay back the murderers and bandits
> what they justly deserve.
> Clear them out from your midst
> make a quick end to slavery!]

Rosenfeld portrays these dead workers as the victims of the capitalist system, but he does not yet lash out at the upper classes.

At this early point in his career still very much under the influence of *haskala* literature, he blames the traditional establishment, those rabbis and religious leaders who "mix up your minds with beliefs." Rosenfeld reanimates the dead workers, and uses their secret knowledge of the absence of an afterlife to refute the false, spiritual promises of "the world to come."
Meeting the dead who reveal secret truths to the living is part of a long literary tradition that can be traced back to the works of Homer, Virgil, and Lucian.[25] This tradition, which Rosenfeld appropriates and extends, was prevalent in nineteenth-century Hebrew and Yiddish *haskala* satire, in works such as Yitzkhak Erter's *Gilgul nefesh* (Transfiguration of Soul), Y. Y. Linetski's *Dos poylishe yingl* (The Polish Boy), Sholem Aleykhem's *Di ibergekhapte briv af der post* (The Letters Stolen from the Mail), and M. L. Lilienblum's *Kehal refa'im* (Congregation of the Dead). Rosenfeld infuses the tradition with pessimism and gloom. Although the dead in earlier works offer positive declarations of life in the "true world," Rosenfeld's dead in "Dream on the Brooklyn Bridge" reinforce the despair of the protagonist.

Rosenfeld worked in New York sweatshops and continued to compose poetry throughout the 1890s. His poetry became sought after in the radical Yiddish press. He published work in the *Arbeter fraynd*; in *Di varheyt* (The Truth), the first Yiddish anarchist newspaper published in New York; in *Der folksadvokat* (The People's Advocate), a New York left-wing weekly that was outspokenly antireligious; and in *Di tsukunft* (The Future),[26] founded as a monthly socialist journal in New York by the Yiddish-speaking section of the Socialist Workers' Party. *Di tsukunft*, with editors like Abraham Cahan and Philip Krantz, would become one of the most prestigious Yiddish periodicals in the United States during this period. Cahan and Krantz had previously edited *Arbeter tsaytung* in its early years. As the first Yiddish social democratic newspaper in America, *Der arbeter tsaytung* is perhaps the most important Yiddish publication. According to the Yiddish literary scholar and lexicographer Zalmn Reyzn: "This newspaper created an era both in the Jewish-American labor movement as well as in Jewish-American journalism and literature; it was the central point for the most significant and influential Yiddish writers in America who were known to their audience almost exclusively through their contributions to this newspaper."[27] Rosenfeld was a steady contributor to *Arbeter tsaytung* for the first few years of the publication's existence, at times contributing one poem per week.[28]

Rosenfeld's Sweatshop poems represent only one portion of his total literary output. In addition to his antireligious and, later, socialistic call-to-arms poetry, he also composed a large corpus of Zionistic works. Political Zionism in the 1890s, however, was still in its infancy and would not officially come of age until the first Zionist conference in 1897. Rosenfeld had almost no outlets in which to publish his "National" poems. Most Yiddish newspapers of the 1890s demanded universalistic works that promoted radical ideologies and addressed the working and living conditions of the proletariat. The left-wing press and its editors, particularly editors like Krantz and Cahan, were ardent anti-Zionists. Zionist publications would only emerge around the turn of the century. In the 1890s, before the official formulation of Labor Zionism, this kind of Jewish-national expression was still anathema, even to mainstream socialism.

Rosenfeld published his second collection in 1890. *Di blumenkete* (The Flower Wreath)[29] collected poems that had originally been printed in *Der folksadvokat* between February and June of that year. Mints and M. Braslavski, the same two men who had edited Rosenfeld's poetry in *Di nyu yorker yidisher folkstsaytung*, also edited *Der folksadvokat*. In *Di blumenkete*, Rosenfeld continues to write about the plight of the immigrant shop worker, but with several significant differences. Instead of chiefly blaming the religious establishment for leading the Jewish workers astray, the poet shifts his focus to what is now the central target of his poetic speakers' opprobrium: the bosses. In addition, there is a decisive shift in the tone of these Sweatshop poems that foreshadows his more mature works. Although still mainly optimistic, the poems of *Di blumenkete* demonstrate the genesis of the pessimism and despair that would consume the poet's later writing.

In "Nakht gedankn" (Night Thoughts), an allusion to the influential poem by Heinrich Heine of the same name,[30] the speaker sits by the seaside at night, quietly thinking and crying. Suddenly, as in other Rosenfeld poems, a group of the dead arise, here out of the storming sea that has been agitated by the tears of the "worker-poet." After urging the protagonist to give up his fight for freedom, they disappear as suddenly as they appeared, and the speaker is left more depressed than before. He quickly spots an approaching ship, to him, an obvious symbol of death.[31] He weighs the idea of swimming out to the ship as he attempts to convince himself that dying is preferable to living—at least in death there is equality. However, before making his final choice, he is distracted by a sound:

Halt op a vayle, kalte shif!
Ikh her, mir dakht glokn klingn—
keytn dakht zikh, her ikh brekhn
un di marsilieze zingn . . .

Mayn herts zi filt on yene tsayt
un tsuhitst zikh shnel in flamen—
kh'fil dikh frayheyt in mayn zele
un lib dikh vi a kind zayn mamen.[32]

[Wait a moment, cold ship!
I hear, it seems, bells ringing—

chains, it seems, do I hear breaking
and the singing of the Marseillaise . . .

My heart feels that time
and quickly ignites in flames—
I feel you freedom in my soul
and love you like a child does his mother.]

Unlike the dead in Rosenfeld's earlier call-to-arms poem "Dream on the Brooklyn Bridge," here the dead do not offer an inspirational message. They serve only to reinforce the worker-poet's despair. Although the poem still ends on a positive note, the depression that pervades Rosenfeld's mature Sweatshop poetry finds its first expression in *Di blumenkete*.

Published in 1893, Rosenfeld's third collection, *Poezyen un lider* (Poems and Songs),[33] comprises seventeen poems. Included are several of his best-known "national" compositions, which, faced with the indifference, even hostility of the left-wing Yiddish press toward literature its editors considered "nationalistic," the poet was obliged to publish in book form. In addressing the long history of Jewish suffering, many of the poems of *Poezyen un lider* hark back to a heroic past in which the Jews lived as a strong and happy nation in their homeland, Israel. The disruptive break in this idyllic existence is *goles* (exile), which the poet cites as the main cause of Jewish unhappiness. To remedy this abnormal situation, his poetic speakers offer a straightforward solution: the return of the Jewish people to the land of Israel and the reestablishment of a united, sovereign state.

One of the book's poems that Rosenfeld preserved in later editions of his collected works is "Der yidisher may" (The Jewish May), a poem referred to by almost all of Rosenfeld's critics. The month of May is the herald of summer, and in Rosenfeld's poetry, it symbolizes the reawakening and rebirth of the world, a time when everyone can enjoy the eternal wonders of nature. There is one person, however, in "The Jewish May," who is sick and weak, who drags his feet and looks only at the ground:

> Yeder blum un yeder tsvaygl
> traybn dakht zikh fun im shpas;
> s'lakht fun im yedvede feygl,
> un der vint—er traybt mit kas.
> Fremd di blumen, fremd di bleter,
> fremd di velt, o fremder may!
> Fremde feygl, fremde geter,
> fremde mentshn, alts farbay![34]

> [Every flower and every little branch
> seem to make fun of him;
> every bird laughs at him,
> and the wind—chases him with anger.
> Strange are the flowers, strange the leaves,
> strange the world, O strange May!
> Strange birds, strange gods,
> strange people, all go by!]

Using a device typical of his sentimental poetics, Rosenfeld repeats certain words for effect. In this case, the speaker relates how nature is not only contrary to Jewish life—a trope of *haskala* literature expressed by nineteenth-century Jewish writers, most notably S. Y. Abramovitch, writing under the pseudonym Mendele Moykher-Sforim—but also conspiratorial against the Jew. Yet this was not always the case: when the Jew was *balebos* (master) of his own land, he was one with nature. In the final stanza, the speaker addresses the Wandering Jew and ends his poem with an optimistic, nationalist message:

> Nit mer veln heydn dume
> yogn, traybn dikh on tsol,

vest nokh zayn di zelbe ume
vi fartsaytn—vi a mol!
Tret fanander nor di steshke
fun dayn altn foterland,
s'glit nokh dort a holeveshke
ba der ayngefalener vant.[35]

[No longer will the dumb heathens
chase, drive you unendingly,
you will again be the same nation
as you were in the old days—as you once were!
Just walk the paths
of your old fatherland,
an ember still burns there
by the fallen wall.]

These proto-Zionist motifs, reflective of Hibbat Zion literature
in nineteenth-century Hebrew, comprise a significant portion of
Rosenfeld's poetic oeuvre. The poems of *Poezyen un lider* demonstrate Rosenfeld's desire to be a national poet, much like the one H.
N. Bialik would become in modern Hebrew literature in the late
1890s. Despite Rosenfeld's aspirations and repeated efforts, however, his national poems are generally mediocre. Most are deriva-
tive of earlier and contemporary Hebrew models and, with few
exceptions, are not among his most lasting works.

In 1897, Rosenfeld published his fourth collection of poems,
Lider bukh (Book of Poems),[36] a clear reference and tribute to Heinrich Heine's widely influential *Buch der Lieder*. As he had with the
previous three collections, Rosenfeld financed the book himself,
this time by selling advance subscriptions. He promised potential
subscribers that, in return for their one dollar, they would receive a
substantial collection of poetry. However, as Rosenfeld writes in
the preface to the book: "A comprehensive collection of my works
would comprise five hundred pages. To publish such a book on

good paper and with good craftsmen, like those who published this volume, would have cost a sea of money; such a book I would not have been able to sell for one dollar."[37]

Lider bukh represents the most significant turning point in Rosenfeld's career. Perhaps not as large as the poet would have liked, it is the most substantial of Rosenfeld's four collections and, more important, shows the poet nearing the peak of his craft. Although previous abstract motifs such as the workers' revolution and the attack on religious fanaticism again appear, Rosenfeld now imbues them with human sentiment and melodrama—his primary mode of communication and a central reason for his great success and large, international audience.

Rosenfeld dedicated this fourth collection to the Harvard literary scholar Leo Wiener. The two men had begun their correspondence before the release of *Lider bukh,* and Rosenfeld had correctly intuited the benefit this relationship would have for his career.[38] In 1898, the prestigious Boston house of Copeland and Day published *Songs from the Ghetto,* a bilingual edition of the poet's works. On one side of each page was Wiener's prose translation of Rosenfeld's poems and on the facing side was the poet's corresponding work, transliterated into the Latin alphabet according to the rules of German orthography. The poems in this book include some of Rosenfeld's best works, such as "In shap" (In the Shop),[39] "A trer afn ayzn" (A Tear on the Iron), "Fartsveyflung" (Despair), and "Di kale fun di berg" (The Mountain Bride).

Wiener, whose history of Yiddish literature would appear one year later, was keenly interested in the poet who would occupy a prominent position in his pioneering monograph. Although Yiddish was for him a side interest, Wiener nevertheless invested much energy in this project. In the preface to this first history of Yiddish literature, he describes his research trip to Eastern Europe in the spring and summer of 1898. Traveling to many of the large and small urban centers of Jewish settlement in Russia and

Poland, the professor visited bookstores and met with numerous Yiddish writers, including S. Y. Abramovitch (Mendele Moykher-Sforim), Yankev Dinezon, A. B. Gotlober, Y. Y. Linetski, Y. L. Perets, Sholem Rabinovitch (Sholem Aleykhem), and Mordkhe Spektor.[40] Already a rising academic celebrity, Wiener would reach the pinnacle of his career with his discovery of Rosenfeld.[41]

On the eve of publication of *Songs from the Ghetto*, Rosenfeld embarked on a promotional tour. He visited synagogues, universities, and communal institutions throughout the Northeast, where he read selections from his poetry, often in Yiddish but also in Wiener's English-language translation. Many of his letters to Wiener, sixty-nine of which are preserved in the poet's collected correspondence, reflect the extent of Rosenfeld's reading engagements between 1897 and 1900 and contain frequent requests for more translated material.

On March 17, 1898, Rosenfeld read to the most prominent and affluent Jewish congregation in New York at this time, the Temple Emmanuel. In a letter dated March 29, he informs Wiener that a reporter from the *New York Journal* at the reading had transcribed some of the poems and printed them in the newspaper. Rosenfeld apologizes profusely, freely admitting that the publication of these works before the release of *Songs from the Ghetto* might well compromise the sales and copyright of the book. In an exaggerated tone typical of both his poetry and his personal correspondence, the poet announces: "I am now lying in bed and am so sick that an hour ago Dr. Alperin was here and wrote me a prescription. I can say that I became sick looking at the damn 'Journal.' "[42] In his next letter to Wiener, Rosenfeld claimed to be so affected by this event that, after his upcoming engagement in Boston, he planned not to perform any more public readings until the publication of *Songs from the Ghetto*.[43] Nevertheless, in April of that year, Rosenfeld recited his works at the Lower East Side College Settlement.[44]

Songs from the Ghetto became a best seller and, two years later, was released in a second, expanded edition.[45] The success of this collection sparked national interest in Rosenfeld and afforded him the popularity he quickly came to depend upon. The Yiddish poet appeared in the American press, and *Songs from the Ghetto* was reviewed by, among others, the well-known American novelist and critic William Dean Howells.[46] Readers responded to Rosenfeld's sentimental and melodramatic portrayal of the Jewish Eastern European immigrant experience, and the poet became a celebrity among a wide American audience. This newfound celebrity led to a lifelong desire to succeed as a poet in the English language, although Rosenfeld's chief literary linguistic vehicle remained Yiddish.[47] Despite his many attempts to write poems in English, most of which ended in popular and critical failure, Rosenfeld did achieve success with the poem "I Know Not Why," published by the *New York Daily Herald* along with accompanying sheet music on June 11, 1899:

I lift mine eyes against the sky,
the clouds are weeping, so am I;
I lift mine eyes again on high,
the sun is smiling, so am I.
Why do I smile? Why do I weep?
I do not know, it lies too deep.
I hear the winds of autumn sigh,
They break my heart, they make me cry;
I hear the birds of lovely spring,
My hopes revive, I help them sing.
Why do I sing? Why do I cry?
It lies so deep, I know not why.

Edmund Clarence Stedman would later include "I Know Not Why" in his prestigious *American Anthology*. Rosenfeld took great pride in this achievement, and according to Mordkhe Dantses, a

Yiddish journalist who knew him well, Rosenfeld carried the clipped page of his poem from Stedman's anthology with him at all times.[48]

Rosenfeld's success as an English-language writer may have been minimal, but his translations and national reputation connected him to a community that helped sustain him. His list of patrons reads like a who's who of wealthy and prominent German Jews in New York. People such as Felix Adler, Louis Marshall, Jacob Schiff, Edwin Seligman, Meyer and Cyrus Sulzberger, and Rabbi Stephen Wise supported Rosenfeld's efforts. They did favors for him and raised money on his behalf with the express purpose of liberating him from sweatshop labor. They saw to it that Rosenfeld received numerous speaking engagements and was invited to read his poems, in English translation, to their large, Reform congregations. Rosenfeld's public readings created publicity for the new book and in themselves served as an important source of income. Encouraged by his success, he quit the sweatshop for good. The poet's German Jewish patrons also helped him in various additional ways. Rabbi Stephen Wise, spiritual leader of the Madison Avenue Synagogue (B'nai Jeshurun), at one point offered Rosenfeld a list of his congregants' addresses so that the publisher of *Songs from the Ghetto* might send them advertisement circulars.[49] In 1898, the money these patrons raised on Rosenfeld's behalf—six hundred dollars of which came from Jacob Schiff alone—not only helped defray the publishing costs of *Songs from the Ghetto,* but also financed the purchase of a grocery store for Rosenfeld, a livelihood far less strenuous than his work in the sweatshops.

Unfortunately, Rosenfeld had no aptitude for the grocery business; on several occasions, he expressed to Wiener his desire to sell the store.[50] In a newspaper interview commemorating the one hundredth anniversary of Rosenfeld's birth, the poet's brother, Joseph, describes Rosenfeld's experience: "Well, he was no grocer. If someone came in and bought three dollars worth of groceries, and paid for it with a ten dollar bill, more often than not they would walk out with seventeen dollars change. Needless to say, he wasn't in the grocery business very long."[51]

Vowing never to return to the sweatshop, the poet tried his hand at several other jobs. In 1898, Edwin Seligman secured a position for him classifying the Judaica collection in the Low Memorial Library at Columbia University.[52] Not long afterward, however, in a letter dated February 14, 1899, he wrote Leo Wiener: "God knows how I hate this dry and tiresome work."[53] He worked at Columbia for less than six months. In May 1899, Rosenfeld embarked upon a new commercial venture, a newsstand, aided by the funds raised on his behalf, mainly by his German Jewish patrons Edwin Seligman and Jacob Schiff. "I have purchased a business," he wrote Wiener on May 14. "Jewish businesses, oh, Jewish livings! An operator, a peddler, a 'news-dealer,' oh, a news dealer!"[54] His letter of July 14 conveys the depression and loneliness that would plague Rosenfeld throughout his life: "As you can see by the return address) I am now in Yonkers. I was forced to leave New York because of my health. I am very sick and weak and I can hardly stand on my two feet. I am writing you these few lines while lying in bed. I lie here forgotten almost by everyone."[55] He sold the newsstand after only a few months.

Rosenfeld's relationships with benefactors such as Seligman and Wiener were sometimes difficult. Thus, at one point in the spring of 1898, he tells Wiener that hearing about "Professor Seligman's personal insult against you woke in me a storm of anger." He assures Wiener that, despite being in the "grips" of the German Jewish community, "in another week or two I will extricate myself from all of their favors."[56] That said, Rosenfeld continued to rely on this community, and particularly on Seligman, for financial help.[57]

When he found that living in Yonkers improved his health, Rosenfeld considered opening up a business there.[58] Instead, as he wrote Wiener in February 1900, he founded a new publication with his former collaborator A. M. Sharkansky, his coeditor on the short-lived *Der ashmeday* (Asmodeus). The new project, entitled *Der pinkes* (The Register), was intended as a quarterly journal. Its overtly nonpartisan credo states: *"Der pinkes* will be a completely innocent publication: free from debates, from prejudices and from taking sides. Our motto is: Peace! Peace with the worker, peace with the boss, peace with religion and peace with the free thinker. Peace with all people and all parties."[59] Although Rosenfeld invited Wiener to contribute to this journal, he never did. *Der pinkes* folded in July 1900 after publishing only two issues, neither of which has survived.

The nonpartisanship of *Der pinkes* reflects the growing division in Rosenfeld's loyalties. He continued to contribute poems to the left-wing—and particularly socialist—Yiddish press, but he also took advantage of new publications. For example, in 1899, Rosenfeld contributed his Zionistic "Der yidisher may" (The Jewish May) to *Der yid* (The Jew), a prestigious, newly founded Russian-Yiddish Zionist weekly based in Krakow, which published some of the best-known Yiddish writers of the times. In 1899 alone, contributors included poets such as A. Liyesin, H. D. Nomberg, S. Frug, and A. Reyzn, as well as prose writers M. Spektor, S. Y. Abramovitch, Y. L. Perets, and Sholem Aleykhem.

After nearly two decades of writing, Rosenfeld had found a venue for his "national" poems. Despite claiming not to mix politics with poetry, he was an active Zionist, attending the fourth Zionist Congress in 1900 as an American delegate. Although not central to the proceedings, Rosenfeld's presence at the congress nevertheless bolstered his reputation in the United States. He began regularly contributing poetry to politically conservative publications such as *Der teglikher herald* (The Daily Herald) in 1901, and the following year, he became involved with *Di yidishe velt* (The Jewish World), a daily founded in June 1902 and published by Louis Marshall, one of Rosenfeld's most famous American Jewish patrons.[60] The expressed purpose of this newspaper was to Americanize Eastern European Jews. While serving as its literary editor from June to December of 1902, Rosenfeld contributed forty-two of his own poems, although most had already been published in the Yiddish press or in one of his four collections. They included "Di svet shap," "Der trern miliyoner" (The Teardrop Millionaire), "Mayse bereyshis" (The Story of Genesis), "Unzer shif" (Our Ship), "Mayn yingele" (My Boy), and "Afn buzm fun yam" (On the Bosom of the Ocean).

At a time when political and ideological lines were being sharply drawn, Rosenfeld was able to publish his poems in a diverse group of publications, a measure of his great talent and wide appeal, and of his calling as a professional poet. Although he personally supported several competing political causes, in particular, socialism and Zionism, he sought to avoid mixing politics with poetry and to show that he was first and foremost a poet, whose political affiliations were personal. Several years later, when the Yiddish literary scholar Kalman Marmor, who was also Rosenfeld's friend, invited the poet to participate in the newly founded Zionist publication *Yidisher kemfer* (Jewish Fighter), the poet responded: "My heart is with your project. 'Jew and Worker' was always my motto. There was a time, however, when people did not understand. Actually, I was cursed and ostracized for 'throwing myself' into 'both sides.' It has taken a quarter of a century for the Jewish worker, the *Jewish fighter* to come to me."[61]

Rosenfeld reached the apex of his popularity in both the Yiddish world and beyond during the first decade of the twentieth century. Translations of his collected poems, often under the title *Songs of the Ghetto*, appeared in many European languages, including Czech, French, German, Hungarian, Polish, Romanian, Russian, and Serbian.[62] Thus, in 1902, the German Jewish Zionist leader Berthold Feiwel translated Rosenfeld's poems into German and published them as *Lieder des Ghetto,* accompanied by elaborate, fascinating illustrations by the well-known Jewish artist Moses Lilien.[63] Rosenfeld's growing international reputation led to an improvement in his financial situation; in March 1903, he purchased a small farm in Spencertown, New York, which he would use as a summer and vacation home for the rest of his life.[64]

Rosenfeld's fortunes continued to rise as the European translations of his poems went into second and sometimes third editions. In 1904, Rosenfeld published his *Gezamlte lider* (Collected Poems), a hefty collection of 122 poems that represent the nucleus of his poetic canon and the source for almost all later critical evaluations of the poet's work. In particular, the first section, "Arbeter un frayhayts-lider" (Worker and Freedom Poems), contains his best and most popular works such as "Der trern miliyoner," "A trer afn ayzn," "Di svet shap," "Mayn yingele," "Mayn ruhe plats" (My Resting Place), "Vuhin?" (Whither?), and "Der leyb" (The Lion).

The poet was at his professional peak and he knew it. In a letter dated December 7, 1904, to the Hebrew poet and translator Dov-Ber Tirkel, Rosenfeld writes: "I smile at the reality that I, more than any other Yiddish writer in the new world, have done more to build our mother tongue and raise the status of the Jewish immigrant on this side of the Atlantic."[65]

Rosenfeld's personal life, however, was about to take an abrupt turn for the worse. In 1905, his only son, Joseph, died of cancer at the age of fifteen.[66] Then, in March 1906, the poet was hospitalized in New York for a stroke that paralyzed the right side of his body and caused a temporary loss of eyesight.[67] In a letter dated May 25, 1906, Rosenfeld's brother desperately appeals to Leo Wiener—Rosenfeld's onetime "savior," with whom the poet had not spoken for more than six years:[68] "The need is great, my brother is paralyzed on the hight [*sic*] half side of his body, and not only can't he write but he must not read even one line printed or written, so acute is his nervousness. Prof. Seligman is not home now, Mr. Jacob Schiff is in Japan, it is hard to tell the consequences even if they were here, it would be best if you used your own knowledge about it. My brother doubts whether the rich Jews would do anything for him, as they all must know his condition through the press, and none of them seem to take any interest in his misfortune. Prof. Seligman's brother, the banker, sent him one hundred dollars and that was about the end of it."[69]

Although there is no record of Wiener's response to this letter, Rosenfeld did receive help from various institutions and individuals. Both Jacob Schiff and Edwin Seligman provided him with monthly stipends.[70] Moreover, several political organizations and newspapers organized funds and collected money for the ailing poet.[71] Rosenfeld also reaped some practical benefits from this publicity. For example, Rabbi A. B. Rhine of the B'nai Brith Lodge of Hot Springs, Arkansas, invited Rosenfeld there to recuperate. Rosenfeld accepted the invitation and, in September 1906, spent two weeks at the lodge.[72]

Rosenfeld's health slowly began to improve, but he still spent much time in bed. His long illness removed him from the public eye. Though not able to write with his own hand, Rosenfeld tells Kalman Marmor in a letter dated March 15, 1907, he has dictated some poetry that has been published in the *Forverts* and *Di tsukunft*.[73] Soon, however, Rosenfeld ceased composing poetry. In mid-1907, rumors began circulating that he had died. On August 2, 1907, the same day Rosenfeld's obituary appeared in *Die Neue National Zeitung* of Vienna, the *Roman-tsaytung* (Novel Newspaper) in Lodz reprinted a letter Rosenfeld had sent to the Vilna *Folkstsaytung*. In his typically melodramatic fashion, the poet writes: "I am alive, though death would be preferable to my present situation . . . loneliness, sorrow on account of blindness, suffering and poverty, my children must sadly suffer from need, trapped in difficulties, eight hundred dollars in debts, fallen into the hands of creditors who took away my little house and threw me and my family into the street. It looks like my wife, my children and I will die of hunger. It is even worse that my supposed death was publicized so that now my few supporters will cease sustaining me."[74] The poet's situation was not as dire as he portrayed it. Rosenfeld was residing in Yonkers, and he still owned his country home in Spencertown.

The stroke left Rosenfeld weak for the balance of his life, but he fully recovered from his paralysis and regained his sight. He was thus well enough to resume his career writing for the Yiddish press. In 1908, he began a six-year stint as a regular contributor to the *Forverts,* where he worked for Abraham Cahan, his former editor at the *Arbeter tsaytung.* Rosenfeld published many items in this newspaper including news articles, poems, and feuilletons. It was in the *Forverts* that he would develop one of his most notable comical characters, "Berl der piskater" (Berl the Foulmouthed).[75] And in 1908, the year the first three volumes of his six-volume collected works were published,[76] Rosenfeld became a United States citizen.

Perhaps the crowning achievement for Rosenfeld in 1908, however, was his tour of Eastern and Central Europe. What began as a trip to the baths of Carlsbad to improve his health quickly blossomed into an impromptu reading tour. During the months following his recital in Carlsbad, Rosenfeld was invited to various European Jewish communities in Germany, Austro-Hungary, and Russian Poland. Sholem Aleykhem, whose reading tour began at the end of May 1908, visited many of the same cities before famously collapsing in the shtetl of Baranovich in late July.[77] Rosenfeld's tour began in July and ended in September, but there is no mention in either writer's letters or memoirs of their meeting during this period. Unlike Sholem Aleykhem, Rosenfeld avoided Russia altogether. He had dodged military draft by quitting the country in 1886, and he likely feared reprisal from the Russian authorities. Despite its limitations, Rosenfeld's tour reestablished his reputation among his international audience, and the *Forverts* prominently published his personal accounts of the trip as he sent them from abroad.[78]

Despite the successes of 1908 and his return to prominence in the Yiddish world following his illness and prolonged silence, Rosenfeld's popularity and stature began to decline. The year before, a group of young Yiddish writers, new immigrants mostly from Russia and Poland, had founded a small journal in New York entitled *Di yugend* (Youth). These new voices signaled the beginning of a new era in American Yiddish literature in the second decade of the twentieth century; they would displace Rosenfeld as the central Yiddish poet. The aesthetic tastes of the Yiddish reading audience were changing. With their motto "Art for art's sake," Di yunge (the Young Ones), as this group came to be called, published their poems, stories, articles, and translations both in the existing Yiddish press and in the new collections and periodicals they founded.[79] They had a keen sense of the American Yiddish literary scene and recognized Rosenfeld's prominence within it. Because they were competing for the same readership, one that Rosenfeld dominated, the members of Di yunge naturally attacked him. Although these attacks tended to focus on Rosenfeld's poetics, some were little more than cruel ad hominem assaults.[80] Thus, in an unsigned piece, the short-lived satiric journal *Der baytsh* (The Whip) sneered: "Morris Rosenfeld's correspondences [in the *Forverts*] have made his audience very curious: they all want to know why he publishes them."[81]

Despite their youth and vigor, Di yunge did not rise to prominence overnight. In 1912, Rosenfeld was still a well-known Yiddish poet who frequently contributed to the most widely read Yiddish newspaper in America, the *Forverts,* which that year published a three-volume edition of Rosenfeld's works.[82] In 1913, cities around the world celebrated the poet's fiftieth year, including a banquet on March 8th at New York's Hotel McAlpin and a celebration in Chicago on December 28th, Rosenfeld's actual birthday.[83]

But soon after these celebrations, Rosenfeld's career began its final decline. Cahan had begun accepting fewer of his pieces, and by the middle of 1914, it was clear to him that Rosenfeld's work was no longer as valuable as it had once been. Replying to Rosenfeld's letter of June 25, 1914, Cahan writes that, though he personally believes the poet's talent is great, he has received complaints "from all sides that there is already too much Rosenfeld."[84] When Cahan finally dismissed him from the *Forverts*, Rosenfeld became bitter. In a letter to Reuven Braynin, the Hebrew and Yiddish writer who edited the Montreal Yiddish newspaper *Der keneder odler* (The Canadian Eagle), Rosenfeld claims that he left the newspaper because Cahan was "a journalistic charlatan, a scoundrel." Furthermore, in the letter's postscript, Rosenfeld encourages Braynin to publish it because "I am writing the absolute truth and the world must know it."[85]

A further setback to Rosenfeld's reputation and the low point in his career was the critical and popular failure of *Dos bukh fun libe* (The Book of Love),[86] a large collection of love poetry that includes Rosenfeld's own Yiddish-language translation of the *Song of Solomon*. In the introduction to the collection, the poet attacks Di yunge by indirectly denigrating their already voluminous poetic efforts: "The true love-poem, the pure, soulful love-poem, does not yet exist in our mother tongue."[87] Past his prime, however, Rosenfeld was writing in a genre that had never been his finest. His love lyrics were weak, and the decision to publish an entire collection in this genre was an unfortunate mistake.

This is not to suggest that Rosenfeld's talent had completely faded away. To the contrary, his poem on the Triangle Shirtwaist Factory fire of 1911, originally published on the front page of the *Forverts*, is one of his most powerful and best Sweatshop poems. Moreover, the satirical poems he composed in the last decade of his life are both biting and amusing. The popularity and critical acclaim of Di yunge, however, pushed Rosenfeld to invest too much of his energy in work that was spiteful and, ultimately, fruitless. Rosenfeld's seemingly overnight fall from grace and his unceremonious dismissal from the most widely read Yiddish daily, of which he was a star writer for several years, gravely wounded the once widely respected poet. On September 27, 1914, Rosenfeld wrote to Yekhezkel Levit, a poet in the mode of Hibbat Zion and the editor of the conservative Boston weekly *Yidishe shtime* (Jewish Voice)—one of the last publications still willing to publish Rosenfeld—threatening not to send any more poetry until he saw all seven of the poems he had already sent Levit in print, and not merely the two that had been published. The emptiness of this threat was reinforced in his next letter to Levit, dated one week later, in which Rosenfeld enclosed two more poems for publication.[88]

No longer published by the left-wing Yiddish press, and finding it increasingly difficult to find venues for his work because of his fiery temperament and his waning poetic stock, Rosenfeld went to work in 1915 for two conservative newspapers with much smaller circulations, the *Tageblat* (Daily Page) and the *Amerikaner* (American). Many of the poems he published in this final stage of his career are sharp satirical attacks against many of the enemies that he had made throughout his life, but he reserved his greatest anger and wrath for Abraham Cahan, with whom he had had an ambivalent relationship since the 1890s. In 1917, Rosenfeld published a series of satirical poems, which he had meant to collect under the title *Di shraybarniye* (The Writers' Gathering Place)[89] along with others still in manuscript form, in the *Yidishe shtime*. In a particularly nasty poem, he makes a clear reference to Cahan, who was cross-eyed, as "Der kosoker soker" (The Cross-eyed Sucker).[90]

In addition to his work in the Yiddish press, Rosenfeld also worked on two other manuscripts. In 1919, he published the first, *Grine tsores un andere shriftn* (Troubles of a Greenhorn and Other

Writings),[91] a collection of two longer humoristic pieces, "Levy in America" and "Rachel in America," and numerous shorter prose pieces gathered into a third section, "Miscellaneous Writings." He also completed work on a second manuscript, "Songs of a Pilgrim," the culmination of his twenty-year effort to create original verse in English. In the last stages of production, however, the publisher informed Rosenfeld that the book would be published only if the young American Jewish poet Louis Untermeyer could edit the manuscript. Terribly insulted, Rosenfeld abandoned the project.[92]

In 1921, Rosenfeld was fired from *Tageblat*, one of the few places where he was still able to publish. The text of his letter of termination reads in its entirety: "Dear Sir: We find it necessary to inform you that from today on you no longer need to write for us. The main reason is that your writing is not good enough in terms of quality and quantity. With Respect, Sarazon and Son."[93] By this point, Rosenfeld was quite ill and rarely left his house in the Pelham Bay section of the Bronx. Di yunge represented the American Yiddish poetic establishment, who were themselves being challenged by a new group of poets known as "In zikh" (Within the Self). Nevertheless, all three generations of writers were represented in the Y. L. Perets Writer's Union, which organized a banquet to celebrate Rosenfeld's sixtieth birthday: "Dear Friends! On Saturday evening, the twenty-sixth of May, in the Central Opera House, 205 East Sixty-Seventh Street, near Third Avenue, there will take place an honor-banquet for our great poet Morris Rosenfeld, who has just turned sixty years old." This invitation is signed by the members of the union's board including writers of Rosenfeld's generation such as Yankev Milkh, Morris Vinchevsky, Avrom Reyzn, and Leon Kobrin, as well as younger Yiddish writers such as Moyshe-Leyb Halpern, Menakhem Boreysho, and H. Leyvik.[94]

Less than one month after this banquet, Morris Rosenfeld died in the early hours of Friday, June 22, 1923. He was at home when he suffered a fatal stroke late on Thursday and died just after midnight. His death and funeral received much attention in both the Yiddish and the American mainstream press.[95] Obituary announcements appeared in the Friday and Saturday newspapers, followed by remembrances and editorial pieces throughout the next week. A month later, after the traditional thirty days of mourning, there was another flurry of articles, and additional pieces were written in the Yiddish press on the anniversaries of his birth and death.[96]

Rosenfeld received his most extensive posthumous coverage in the newspaper where he had worked as a reporter, editor, essayist, and poet for over ten years, the *Forverts*. In the Friday edition, Rosenfeld's death was announced in a large front-page article with his picture. The following day, another front-page article detailed the plans for the poet's funeral, and, on the editorial page of this issue, Cahan eulogized the poet in generous terms: "In Morris Rosenfeld there lived the divine spark through which true art was created. He was a poet. Upon each corner of life which he threw his glance, he saw with the eyes of a poet."[97]

According to another front-page article in the *Forverts*, this one on Monday, June 25, 1923, the day after Rosenfeld's funeral, crowds began gathering at the undertaker's building at eight A.M. Hundreds of people accompanied the body from East Fifth Street near Second Avenue, to the office of the *Forverts* on East Broadway. There Rosenfeld was eulogized from nine A.M. until noon by prominent Yiddish literary figures such as Morris Vinchevsky, Leon Kobrin, Reuven Braynin, Alexander Harkavy, Avrom Reyzn, Kalman Marmor, and Menakhem Boreysho. At noon, the procession to the cemetery began. The crowd made its way on foot from the *Forverts* office, over the Williamsburg Bridge into Brooklyn, and then up to the Mount Carmel Cemetery. It was estimated that a total of twenty-five thousand people attended these ceremonies, one of the largest crowds ever to attend a Jewish funeral in New York.[98]

2

The Appropriation of Morris Rosenfeld

Morris Rosenfeld published his fourth collection of poems, *Lider bukh* (Books of Poems), in September 1897. The first critical response to the poet's work appeared that November in *Der nayer gayst* (The New Spirit), a monthly nonpartisan forum for the best and most promising Yiddish literature and scholarship of the day, edited by the well-known Yiddish scholar and linguist Alexander Harkavy.

Writing in the journal's second issue, L. Budianov (Louis Budin), a young Russian Jewish journalist who had immigrated to the United States six years earlier, attacks Rosenfeld in "A Poet Led Astray."[1] Budianov finds Rosenfeld's national poetry—in which the poet has invested much energy—without feeling and contrived. Moreover, "the difference between Rosenfeld as he is and Rosenfeld the way Rosenfeld considers himself, this dualism in Rosenfeld's nature between his heart and his head, colors all of his poetry."[2] Budianov criticizes the popular conception of Rosenfeld as a "folk poet" and argues that the term is antiquated. When people identify with a class rather than with a nation, every poet, Budianov suggests, becomes a "class poet." Furthermore, Rosenfeld's Sweatshop poetry is not specifically Jewish, but working-class; he is a worker's poet. Whereas Rosenfeld's Zionist poetry is clichéd and outdated, his "practical" and "universal" proletarian

31

poems, as products of Rosenfeld's personal experience, are more valuable.

By challenging Rosenfeld's supposed folk status, Budianov demonstrates both that Rosenfeld's poetry was well known to Yiddish readers and that, at least in certain literary circles, he was considered a poet of the people. At a time when the notion of the "national" writer was quickly gaining currency in Jewish literature, Budianov voices his own decidedly socialist position. By harnessing Rosenfeld's poetry to the international workers' cause, he attempts to universalize the poet and thereby deny him national status.

Budianov's critique was countered in the next issue of *Der nayer gayst* by the once widely popular Yiddish writer Leon Kobrin.[3] In "A Critique Led Astray," Kobrin argues that, because Rosenfeld's poetry focuses on Eastern European Jewry and, specifically, on the Eastern European Jewish worker, Rosenfeld is neither a universal nor a worker's poet. Moreover, if Rosenfeld is also not a national poet, it is only because the Jews do not constitute a nation.[4] Contrary to Budianov's contention, however, Rosenfeld is indeed a folk poet, and a fine one.

In his two-part response to Kobrin,[5] the Yiddish author and literary editor Yankev Milkh raises issues central to the Rosenfeld debate. "Does Rosenfeld's poetry mirror something of the Jewish character?" he asks. "Is there something particularly Jewish about his poetry? And, if so, what does this specifically Jewish character consist of?"[6] Milkh attempts to reconcile the two previously stated views: Rosenfeld is a worker's poet who reflects the suffering and hopes of the working class in the mother tongue of Eastern European Jews.

The position of Yiddish as the vernacular of Eastern European Jewry encouraged the development of Yiddish literature, a benefit not enjoyed by its Hebrew counterpart, but it came with a price. However natural a literary vehicle Yiddish may seem from our twenty-first-century perspective, Eastern European Jews of the late nineteenth and early twentieth centuries saw the situation differently. As Dan Miron shows,[7] most Eastern European Jews considered Yiddish a debased *zhargon* (jargon), unfit for literary expression. This sentiment was shared by many Yiddish writers of the time, Miron notes, including notables such as S. Y. Abramovitch, Sholem Aleykhem, and Y. L. Perets—authors whose careers lasted into the second decade of the twentieth century, through the years when Rosenfeld was in the prime of his career and the Yiddish press was in its first flowering. Yiddish was held to be, not a national language, but a language of the masses. As such, writers such as Rosenfeld and Sholem Aleykhem were considered "folk" writers, employing the language and reflecting the lives of the masses in their work; Yiddish literature as a whole was considered a "folk" literature created for a simple and poorly educated audience. By definition, a folk writer could not be a sophisticated artist. Although Hebrew embodied certain key Romantic aspects of the Jewish nation—its past, psyche, and myths—Yiddish was the language of the uneducated masses, which, at best, related current events through the press and through propagandistic verse. The designation of "folk poet" thus served to relegate the achievements of Yiddish writers such as Rosenfeld to a subliterary standing of limited importance.

The debate over Rosenfeld in *Der nayer gayst* roughly coincided with the poet's new friendship with Leo Wiener, the Harvard professor who would be largely responsible for Rosenfeld's breakthrough success in the non-Yiddish world. The 1898 publication of the bilingual *Songs from the Ghetto,* which included Wiener's English translation of the poet's works, generated much critical writing on Rosenfeld, especially in America. Indeed, this book and its reception set the tone for Rosenfeld's growing relationship with the affluent German Jewish community of New York, which maintained a patronizing attitude toward both the poet and the immigrant world he represented.

Such an attitude dominated critical treatments of Rosenfeld's poetry in the American press of the period. The reviews of *Songs from the Ghetto,* though for the most part positive, treat Yiddish as a literary curiosity, sometimes even a barbaric one. Writing for the literary journal *The Bookman,* the well-known American journalist I. F. Marcosson compares Wiener's translation favorably to "the original 'Yiddish,' " which he characterizes as "a guttural chant, often irritating, never attractive."[8] In an even more disdainful tone, "lest the name of Yiddish terrify our readers overmuch,"[9] *The Dial* assures them that Wiener's translations make *Songs from the Ghetto* palatable. These and other reviews portray Rosenfeld as an uneducated worker who managed to rise above his situation through the redeeming muse of poetry, and it is his status as a genuine Lower East Side immigrant that proves crucial to his literary acceptance.[10]

European critics appropriated Rosenfeld's poetry in a similar manner. Publishers produced a number of European translations of Rosenfeld's works during the first decade of the twentieth century, basing most of them on Wiener's English translation; many even maintained the title *Songs from the Ghetto.*[11] In his introduction to *Lieder des Ghetto,* Berthold Feiwel, the German Jewish Zionist leader who translated the volume into German, emphasizes that Rosenfeld is not a sophisticated littérateur: "He writes what he lives. No foreign literature offered him a matrix for his poetry. No master taught him verse and rhyme: an old tailor's soul, he was a hungry Jew who became a poet during sleepless nights, without him wanting or realizing it—through the hard trials of dire need."[12] Feiwel argues that Rosenfeld is not a poet in the ordinary sense of the word but, rather, a kind of Jewish Everyman who translates his life into poetry.

One of the most significant critical works to come out of the European interest in Yiddish—an interest that Rosenfeld helped spark—is the ambitious 1910 dissertation on the history of Yiddish literature by the French scholar Meyer Isser Pinès.[13] Pinès dedicates a large section of "Histoire de la littérature judéo-allemande" to Rosenfeld, complete with literal French translations of many of his poems. His selection and focus—based on the second edition of *Shriftn* (Writings; 1906) and divided accordingly into the Sweatshop poems (Pinès's largest subsection), followed by the national, the lyrical, and the satirical poems—belie Pinès's definition and perception of Rosenfeld as a poet. Like the American critics, Pinès locates Rosenfeld's talent in his personal experience as a worker, thereby establishing him as a proletarian writer whose poetry expresses the collective through the personal. As the renowned critic Bal Makhshoves (Isidore Eliyashev) notes in his introduction, the Yiddish translation of the Pinès opus represents the first book-length history of Yiddish literature in Yiddish.[14]

Mainstream Yiddishist critics such as Sh. Niger, Borukh Rivkin, Nakhman Meisel, and Avrom Tabachnik would also perpetuate the notion of Rosenfeld as a poet of the collective experience. In the first decade of the twentieth century, when Rosenfeld's popularity was reaching its peak, Yiddish literary criticism was still in its infancy. Sh. Niger, one of the first professional Yiddish critics and a proponent of high art, whose influential opinions became the accepted standard, concentrated his efforts on educating the Yiddish reader. He preferred the works of writers such as Y. L. Perets, whom he considered a sophisticated artist, and labeled authors such as Rosenfeld and Sholem Aleykhem, whose work he found primitive, "folk" writers.

For Niger, Rosenfeld was a mediocre poet whose best and only lasting poems were those where he simply described, in dramatic fashion, the life he experienced while employed in sweatshops. Writing in 1913 on the double occasion of Rosenfeld's fiftieth birthday and the publication of the latest volumes of his collected works, Niger appreciates the emotional intensity of Rosenfeld's poem "Mayn yingele" (My Boy), saying that it "could move a stone."[15] But he dismisses Rosenfeld's later Sweatshop poems—those written in the first decades of the twentieth century when Rosenfeld was no longer a sweatshop worker—as weak and unconvincing.[16]

Borukh Rivkin takes a more sociological approach. Although Niger believes that the task of writers is to elevate their readership, Rivkin emphasizes the influence of the readership on the writers' creative process. He portrays Rosenfeld as a sweatshop worker who emerged from the *oylem* (people), and who, in response to the demands of his immigrant readers, expressed their common experiences in a simple, accessible poetic form. For Rivkin, rudimentary socialism, though certainly present in Rosenfeld's early poems, is important only to the extent that it gave Rosenfeld his start. Far from being a politically tendentious poet who wrote only in definite genres such as the national or the proletarian, Rosenfeld was in fact a product of his time, engaging ideologies—such as Zionism and socialism—because they appealed to the masses that made up his audience. Rosenfeld's poetry was tailor-made for his readers.[17]

Contrary to Niger, however, Rivkin sees Rosenfeld's authenticity not as detracting from his groundbreaking accomplishments in American Yiddish poetry, but rather as an integral part of his artistic development. He credits Rosenfeld with being both the first to bring certain poetic forms into Yiddish literature and the first American Yiddish writer to develop the poet in himself. Still it is his authentic status, his connection to *amkho* (the simple Jewish people), that Rivkin considers Rosenfeld's chief poetic asset. A quasi-organic unity between the poet and his audience shaped and helped to create his poetry. But when, with Di yunge and the rise of Yiddish literary modernism, Yiddish readers grew more sophisticated, Rosenfeld, a product of his social-historical context, could not adapt to their more literarily advanced tastes. This, for Rivkin, is further proof of his authenticity.

In the essay that introduces his book *Dikhter un dikhtung* (Poets and Poetry), Avrom Tabachnik divides Rosenfeld's poetry into *shtil* (quiet) and *shturmish* (stormy). He quickly dismisses the "quiet" poems: "However good, pure and melodic these quiet poems may be, they are far from the most important in Rosenfeld's oeuvre. Other poets of Rosenfeld's generation could have luckily stumbled upon and written such warm, folksy-melodic poems as 'Mayn yingele,' or such Heine-like poems such as 'Der kanarik' (The Canary)."[18] Tabachnik prefers Rosenfeld's "stormy" poems, stressing their unique nature and importance: "But no other poet besides Rosenfeld could have, in the 1890s, achieved the style of 'The Sweatshop,' 'Ershter may' (May the First), 'Afn buzim fun yam'(On the Bosom of the Ocean)."[19]

Tabachnik considers these poems Rosenfeld's best and most important not simply because they are stylistically sophisticated or "stormy," but because they contain "a more complicated, deeper social-historical meaning—that which later emerged in him under the influence of his time and its characteristic ideas, conflicts and goals."[20] Like Rivkin, Tabachnik sees Rosenfeld's poems as reflecting and embodying his time and place. As so many other critics, he cites the poet's authenticity as the main criterion for his poetic greatness, indeed, as what distinguishes him from other Sweatshop poets such as Yoysef Bovshover, Dovid Edelshtat, and Morris Vinchevsky, with whom Rosenfeld is commonly classified in Yiddish criticism. After dismissing Bovshover and Edelshtat as "bohemian" and "not very creative," respectively, Tabachnik states that the main reason Rosenfeld is a great poet and Vinchevsky is not is that "whereas Vinchevsky *went* to the masses, Rosenfeld *came* from the masses."[21]

For leading Yiddishist critic and literary historian Nakhman Meisel,[22] it is Rosenfeld's experience as a sweatshop worker who suffered along with the toiling immigrant masses that lends his poetry credibility: "He himself endured all the tortures of hell."[23] Moreover, Rosenfeld's Sweatshop poems are superior to his national ones, which "do not originate from his own personal depths."[24]

Rosenfeld is at his best, writes noted Yiddish commentator Sol Liptzin, when he "deals with personal experiences and communicates feelings. [On the other hand,] Rosenfeld's Zionist songs lack the concrete imagery and the sense of immediacy which his sweatshop poems, based on real personal experiences, possess."[25]

In a chapter appropriately titled "Morris Rosenfeld—Sweatshop Poet," literary historian Charles Madison, a contemporary of Liptzin, likewise suggests that Rosenfeld's best poems "are genuinely the direct expression of the worker."[26] But when he claims that, being "written in a simple but idiomatic Yiddish,"[27] Rosenfeld's poems mirror his life even on a linguistic level, Madison's critique goes awry. As I shall demonstrate in chapter 4, Rosenfeld wrote many of his poems, particularly the Sweatshop poems so important to Madison, in a Yiddish that is both nonidiomatic and highly contrived.

American and Yiddish critics alike insist on authenticity as the yardstick to measure Rosenfeld's literary success. The American critics apologize to their readers for Rosenfeld's artless and simple poetry, but they argue that Rosenfeld's life experiences redeem his poetry as a genuine representation of the working classes. The Yiddish critics argue that, because Rosenfeld lived the life he portrayed, his poetry has an element of truth, which gives it value. Despite their varied conclusions about the effect Rosenfeld's authenticity had on his poetry, all the critics agree on one thing: Rosenfeld was intimately tied to his audience.

As literary scholars have noted, a promodernist tendency dominated the criticism of American literature following the rise of the New Critics. The critical establishment, beginning in the 1930s, held up poets such as T. S. Eliot and Ezra Pound as examples of American poetry at its best.[28] The same modernist aesthetic came to dominate Yiddish literary criticism, particularly in defin-

ing the putative canon of American Yiddish poetry. The current
Yiddish literary establishment—contemporary scholars, as well as
the editors of the recent English-Yiddish poetic anthologies—have
only reinforced these promodernist tastes. We can trace the genesis of this consensus to the opinions of Di yunge (the Young Ones),
the self-professed American Yiddish modernists. With poetic sensibilities tending toward neo-Romanticism and symbolism, Di
yunge formed a negative opinion of Rosenfeld that prevails in Yiddish literary criticism to this day. Ironically, it would be the true
proponents of high modernism in Yiddish, writers such as Yankev
Glatshteyn, A. Leyeles, and Nokhem Borekh Minkov, who would
reevaluate Rosenfeld in a positive manner and appreciate him
within the context of their own modernist sensibilities.

During the second decade of the twentieth century, as Di
yunge rose to literary prominence, the changing aesthetic tastes of
the Yiddish reading public began to displace Rosenfeld as a central
Yiddish poet. The older writer clearly understood that his position
was under attack, and he confronted his opponents publicly, as he
had in the past. One of the first pieces Rosenfeld addressed to Di
yunge was a feuilleton he published in the *Forverts*: "Berl the Foulmouthed Becomes a Decadent." [29] Rosenfeld had created this character as "Berl the Proletarian" four years earlier in the pages of the
Forverts. At first a comic quasi poet who delights in rhyming almost anything, Berl soon falls under the influence of a pernicious
literary movement of young poets on the Lower East Side and becomes a "decadent" who focuses upon writing *shtimungs poeziye*
(the poetry of feeling or mood) and Impresionizm (impression-
ism). This reference is an obvious jibe at Di yunge, who valued
shtimung as a central poetic tenet, and who were among the first
American Yiddish writers to experiment with literary impression-
ism. Rosenfeld, speaking in the poem in the first person, states that
he is afraid to enter the café where Berl holds forth. He fears that
Berl and his decadent compatriots—in his opinion, opponents of

literal speech—will attack him as an enemy of art. An example of Berl's poetry serves as the feuilleton's epigraph:

> Nider mit di alte dikhter!
> Ver ken zey atsind fartrogn?
> Filn, zey zaynen vos zey zogn,
> Fuy! Zey zaynen undz tsu nikhter.
> Nit keyn khshad un nit keyn roykh,
> un di velt farshteyt zey oykh.
>
> [Down with the old poets!
> Who can stand them today?
> They feel, they are what they say,
> Yuck! They are too sober for our taste.
> No smoke and no hint,
> and, moreover, the audience understands them.]

Rosenfeld is sending a clear message to Di yunge in the pages of the most widely read Yiddish publication of the time. In an ironic tone, which often crosses over to pure sarcasm, he mocks what he perceives to be their pretensions and poetic shortcomings.

It did not take long for a member of the opposing camp to counterattack. Two weeks after the publication of Rosenfeld's poem, Moyshe-Leyb Halpern, a twenty-four-year-old poet who had begun his career only a few years before, published "An Open Letter to Morris Rosenfeld"[30] in the pages of *Der kibitzer*, a satiric periodical with which he was closely involved.[31] Halpern compares Rosenfeld to a mechanical amusement park clown, a popular attraction he had seen in Vienna years before. When someone fed the clown a coin and pushed its "pig" button, it would roll around on the ground and squeal, to the delight of onlookers. One year later, however, this same clown had become rusty and neglected by the crowd; now when someone fed it a coin, it would roll around, but it no longer had the ability to squeal. Halpern's biting allegory is multifaceted. The once popular poetic voice of Rosenfeld, likened at its best to the pig's squeal of a clown rolling in the mud, can through neglect no longer even be heard; the poet himself has become an almost forgotten oddity. That the clown performs only when fed a coin alludes to the claim by many of the younger writers that the older, more established Yiddish authors, particularly Rosenfeld and Sholem Asch, were more interested in making money than in making art. Halpern's essay, however, is more extreme than the typical pronouncements made by the members of this younger generation and represents, as we shall see below, but one side of Moyshe-Leyb Halpern's ambivalent relationship to Rosenfeld and his work.

Di yunge were a loose aggregate of writers who, despite their consensus on Rosenfeld, often agreed on little else. In their journals and anthologies, they published original fiction and poetry as well as translations from world literature; they set forth their general demands of literature in several theoretical pieces. Thus the ambitious 1915 anthology *Fun mentsh tsu mentsh* (From Person to Person), which Halpern edited, contains both the works of many of Di yunge's central writers—poetry by A. M. Dilon, H. Leyvik (Leyvik Halper), Mani Leyb (Brahinski), and Menakhem (Boreysho) and prose by L. Shapiro, Ayzik Raboy, Yoysef Opatoshu, and Dovid Ignatov[32]—and a short theoretical essay by Reuven Ayzland, soon to become the chief theoretician and poetic spokesman of Di yunge.

Tastes in American Yiddish poetry had already begun to change, Ayzland writes in "The New Tendency in Yiddish Poetry."[33] Although earlier theoretical pieces published in Di yunge's previous publications, such as *Di yugend* (Youth) or the ambitious *Shriftn* (Writings),[34] had encouraged a change in literary tastes, Ayzland's essay in *Fun mentsh tsu mentsh* treats Di yunge's poetic principles—especially, the importance of individual experience and mood in poetry—as a fait accompli in the Yiddish world. He criticizes older Yiddish poetry for its supposed lack of mood and for its reliance on prefabricated ideas and expressions—implying but not naming Rosenfeld's poetry. Writing a year after the publishing failure of *Dos bukh fun libe* and Rosenfeld's dismissal from the *Forverts* seems to have given Azyland confidence in presenting Di yunge's new literary aesthetic.

The anxiety Rosenfeld engendered in the later writings of Di yunge, especially evident in the anthology *Di yidishe dikhtung in amerike biz yor 1919* (Yiddish Poetry in America Up to the Year 1919), is clear testimony to Rosenfeld's immense stature in Yiddish literature. Zisho Lande—a poet who came closest to a pure expression of Di yunge's tenets in his poetry—edited the volume, which includes four poems by Rosenfeld. Lande's appraisal of pre-Di yunge poetry in America can be summed up in two well-known quotations from his introduction: "The national and social movements each had their own rhyme departments," and "The history of Yiddish poetry until the beginning of this century is itself the history of an episode in the labor movement."[35]

Lande states that, despite its title, his anthology is not specifically a historical survey. To collect materials for the book, he "looked through Yiddish poetry, first and foremost, for the live, unmediated word."[36] To understand what Lande meant by "the live, unmediated word," we must look carefully at both the poets he chose to include and those he chose to ignore, as well as at how he canonized his selections.

Of the four Rosenfeld poems, only the first, "Valt Vitman" (Walt Whitman), is not an excerpt from a longer poem. Lande takes his second from Rosenfeld's Zionistic "Yeshaye" (Isaiah), which he expressly identifies as an excerpt, entitling it "From Isaiah." Rooted in oppositions and predicated on the arrival of the Messiah when these oppositions will be resolved, "Isaiah" is a long, repetitive poem based on the prophecies of the biblical prophet:

Yo, blien, blien, freyen zikh un zingen,
levonen's herlikhkeyt vet dort erklingen,
di sheynheyt fun dem karmel un fun shoren.[37]

[Yes, [they will] bloom, bloom, celebrate and sing.
Lebanon's gloriousness will resound there,
the beauty of Carmel and Sharon.]

Rosenfeld wrote a number of poems in this effusive, nine-teenth-century style, contributing to the relatively small corpus of Hibbat Zion poetry in Yiddish. Lande extracts only ten lines from "Yeshaye," and he creates his own ending by inventing a final line, which he repeats:

Di blinde velen zen, di toybe hern.
Der lomer, vi a hirsh vet damols shpringn,
der tsung fun shtumn, zise lider zingen.
Un kvaln in di viste trikenishn.
Un kvaln in di viste trikenishn.[38]

[The blind will see, the deaf hear,
The lame one will then leap like a deer,
the tongue of the silent one will sing sweet songs.
And springs [will flow] in the desolate dry lands.
And springs in the desolate dry lands.]

Not only has Lande redrawn the poem's original Zionist con-text; he has also imposed on it a quality of terseness that is present in much of his own poetry, particularly his early, short lyrics. Cen-tral to the style of Hibbat Zion is its expressive loquacity. Lande's appropriation of "Yeshaye" and "In zayn hand" (In His Hand),[39] offers readers misinformed and decontextualized versions of Rosenfeld's poems. For the fourth Rosenfeld selection, he has cre-ated a title, "Zunenlikht un lerkhe klang" (Sunlight and the Sound of Larks), for an originally untitled section of the poem cycle "Friling" (Spring).

Lande has chosen poems that have a thematic unity and that present oppositions, itself a central motif in Lande's own poetry and one he emphasizes in Rosenfeld's through excerption. Rosenfeld is the only poet of his generation to be included in an anthology with the major and minor poets of Lande's cohort. Lande could not simply ignore the older poet, as he does Rosenfeld's contemporaries such as Bovshover, Edelshtat, and Vinchevsky. Instead, however, he appropriated him—by re-creating his poems within the context of Lande's own poetics.

This need to address the poet who played such a prominent role in the development of Yiddish poetry in America finds a more balanced expression in Moyshe-Leyb Halpern's 1915 essay "The Old and the New Morris Rosenfeld,"[40] which addresses Rosenfeld's failed *Dos bukh fun libe.* Unlike his earlier, "Open Letter" attack, Halpern's consideration of Rosenfeld here is more nuanced; he contextualizes the older poet as a product of his time. Predictably, Halpern rejects the "new" Rosenfeld of the love lyric as old-fashioned and inept. His comments, however, on the "old" Rosenfeld are insightful and reveal how the "old" Rosenfeld's poetics intersect with those of Di yunge.

As several critics have noted, Halpern was a peripheral member of Di yunge, not one of its mainstays. The group was never a completely coherent unit; after several years, its most talented members developed unique styles and went their own literary ways. Poets such as Reuven Ayzland and Zisho Lande remained more aligned with the central tenets of Di yunge, whereas other, more talented and individual poets such as Halpern or H. Leyvik, who began their careers in association with Di yunge, quickly departed on their own poetic paths.

One overwhelming element in Halpern's poetry is his insistence on—perhaps even obsession with—the truth, a concern that dominates his entire oeuvre. Focusing on the "old" Morris Rosenfeld, Halpern explains that it was impossible for the older poet, writing two decades before, to create "art for art's sake"—as the central tenet of Di yunge's poetics demanded—because this concept did not yet exist in Yiddish poetry. Rosenfeld's aesthetic merits thus cannot be judged by the same criteria with which modern poets evaluate contemporary poetry. As Borukh Rivkin would argue some years later, Rosenfeld wrote for a literarily immature audience and thus embodied the highest expression of its aims and ideas "because he was its flesh and blood."[41]

Like many of the Yiddish poets of his generation, Halpern was greatly influenced by Rosenfeld. Yiddish poetry in America, if it did not begin with Rosenfeld himself, certainly began with his generation. Morris Rosenfeld was the most talented poet of his era, a fact that Di yunge clearly understood and could not avoid. Of his literary generation, it was Halpern who had the most complex relationship with the older poet's works, and in his essay, his affection for Rosenfeld is clear, particularly in his appraisal of what he considers to be the poet's best works, his Sweatshop poems.

Here, Halpern writes, Rosenfeld rises above the poets of his generation "like a roaring lion among mewing cats," particularly in a poem such as "The Sweatshop": "We feel like these are words which have been made to glow in the heart of the protest-poet, like pieces of iron in the wild fire of a blacksmith."[42] Readers familiar with Halpern's poems can begin to see here his literary identification with Rosenfeld. Halpern, whose middle name, "Leyb," means lion, often presents his persona as "Moyshe Leyb," which, although among the most common of traditional Ashkenazi names, can also be understood as "Moyshe the Lion."[43] Furthermore, the raging voice he celebrates in Rosenfeld reflects his own anger, an anger that often becomes an incoherent rage in his later poems, specifically those published posthumously.

Halpern demonstrates his admiration for Rosenfeld in the disappointed tone of his brief analysis of the poem "Di farfirte" (Led Astray). Unlike the pure anger of his "Open Letter," or his dismissal of the "new" Rosenfeld, Halpern pushes for more truth in this poem, which describes the seduction of a sweatshop girl by her boss's son. Halpern considers the central incident of the poem too rare and sensationalistic: "The real life of the Jewish shop girl is as rich in images as there are waves in the ocean. The true artist need do no more than just open his eyes, and the images will fly by like flocks of white doves under a clear morning sky. And the true artist need do no more than merely let his light shine over these images."[44]

Halpern demands, not authenticity, as the first group of Rosenfeld's critics did, but truth in art—an idea that Halpern insisted upon both in his own and in others' poetry. Although he is willing to excuse Rosenfeld for certain poetic deficiencies, which he attributes to the older poet's being a product of his time and place, truth in art for Halpern is nevertheless an indispensable criterion of literature that transcends these environmental constraints.

Halpern's own relationship to Rosenfeld demonstrates his distance from the general poetics of Di yunge. Lande's reworking Rosenfeld's poems to fit with his own poetic style, specifically reflecting the younger poet's belief in terseness and restraint, highlights what Lande and others of his generation found objectionable in Rosenfeld's poetry, namely, its loquacity and seemingly uncontrolled effusiveness. Among this younger generation, who relegated Rosenfeld to the status of a propagandistic and premodern poet, it was only Halpern who cogently understood—and stated—that Rosenfeld was a product of his environment, a pioneer poet creating a poetic with almost no modern, literary tradition on which he could model his poetry.

The generation of Di yunge, emerging as it did at the time of Rosenfeld's greatest popularity, could not avoid directly confronting the older poet. When, however, the next literary generation came to the fore in American Yiddish literature, Rosenfeld, well past his prime, had become a tragic figure, not a force with which the new generation had to reckon. Organized around the journal *In zikh* (Within the Self), whose name they adopted, these young writers and poets of the 1920s viewed Rosenfeld from a more generous perspective. They reevaluated the older poet, according him a more prominent position in American Yiddish poetry than the one to which he had been relegated by the previous literary generation.

The chief proponent of Rosenfeld's rehabilitation was Nokhem Borekh Minkov, a prominent poet and critic associated with In zikh. In Minkov's 1937 *Yidishe klasiker poetn* (Classic Yiddish Poets), he presents Rosenfeld as one of the "classic" poets of Yiddish.[45] Minkov endows Rosenfeld with the credibility and pedigree of the three canonized prose writers of modern Yiddish literature, S. Y. Abramovitch, Sholem Aleykhem, and Y. L. Perets. Minkov deliberately avoids classifying Rosenfeld as a "pioneer" of Yiddish literature, the strategy of other critics, who had used this designation to relegate the older poet's accomplishments to merely historical significance. Instead, Minkov explicitly states that Rosenfeld is a chief representative of the mature American Yiddish poetry, to which these pioneer poets are precursors. In the introduction to his seminal multivolume study of early American Yiddish poetry *Pionern fun der yidisher poeziye in amerike* (Pioneers of Yiddish Poetry in America; 1956), he argues that, although Rosenfeld began his career as a pioneer, both in tone in time, he "crossed the border of the era,"[46] and thus deserves the title of "classic."

Rosenfeld is at his best, argues Minkov, when he contains his wild, poetic energy and harnesses it within a stable poetic form, as he does in "Far vos ikh bin ikh" (Why I am I), in which the speaker, a self-declared poet, addresses his muse:

Ikh hob getray gefolgt dayn ruf,
mayn himls heylike nekhome!
Es hot nokh keynmol nit der guf
bahersht dem shvung fun mayn neshome.

[I have faithfully obeyed your call,
my heaven's holy solace!
Never has my body
overcome the force of my soul.]

Minkov appreciates not only the poet's control but also his awareness of the battle between body and soul within him. This type of self-awareness is a key component in the poetics of In zikh, which is given further elaboration in the critical writings of Yankev Glatshteyn, the dominant figure and central poet associated with this group.

In his 1956 review of Rosenfeld's recently published correspondence, Glatshteyn seems to accept Di yunge's verdict on the poet, describing Rosenfeld as a minor poet who wrote "approximately ten good poems, and four or five great ones."[47] In his 1962 essay honoring the one hundredth anniversary of the poet's birth,[48] however, Glatshteyn praises the neglected poet. Having taken a closer look at Rosenfeld's works, he recants the statements he had made in his earlier article.[49] He now calls Rosenfeld "the most original poet of his generation," "the first Yiddish poet to understand America," and "the father of American Yiddish poetry,"[50] although he is careful to limit Rosenfeld's greatness and innovation to only one of the several modes in which he wrote—the lyrical.

Directly contradicting Di yunge's conclusion that Rosenfeld's lyrical poetry is filled with clichés and prefabricated ideas., Glatshteyn concentrates in large part on Rosenfeld's rarely cited "Kinder libe" (Love for a Child), based on the death of the poet's fifteen-year-old son.

Di gantse velt farshvint in shatn,
vos iz di mentshheyt mit ir noyt
antkegn khurbn fun a tatn,
vos klogt af zayn ben yokhids toyt?[51]

[The entire world disappears in hurt,
what is humanity with its need
when compared to the devastation of a father
who laments his only son's death?]

Rosenfeld's introspection is of crucial value to the central poet of the In zikh school. He clearly appreciates the specific theme of this poem, namely, the discrepancy between the speaker and the world around him. Although it may seem obvious that a parent will feel the pain of the loss of a child more acutely than any other, Glatshteyn appreciates the direct, sincere, and mature self-knowledge of this poem. Referring also to other lesser-known poems such as "Bam breg vaser" (By the Waterside) and "Der mond un ikh" (The Moon and I), Glatshteyn makes the first coherent argument in Yiddish literary criticism that there is much of value in Rosenfeld's lyrical poetry. His position is particularly convincing because he insists—as do several of the aforementioned critics—that Rosenfeld must be understood and appreciated within the proper social, literary, and historical contexts.

Although Rosenfeld received brief recognition and an outpouring of sympathy from the Yiddish press immediately following his death, the dominant view of the poet within the Yiddish critical establishment remained a negative one. It was not until Minkov's serious treatment of Rosenfeld's poetry in 1937, and his reiteration of these views in 1956, that the poet began to be reconsidered in a positive light. Minkov, however, was almost alone in his praise and recognition of the poet. Glatshteyn does not present an especially positive review of Rosenfeld's career in his brief essay of 1956; it is only in 1962 that he revises his position.

Arguably the most influential figure in American Yiddish poetry, Glatshteyn was a talented and educated thinker whose efforts were among the most sophisticated poetic achievements in Yiddish. Many scholars of Yiddish literature, particularly the contemporary ones who have played a fundamental role in attempts at determining a Yiddish canon, hold him in high esteem. It is thus significant to note that, despite the central position Glatshteyn's poetry occupies in this canon, his reevaluation of Rosenfeld seems to have had little, if any, effect on Yiddish scholarship.

The most significant European scholarship on the poet emerged in the Soviet Union during the interwar period. Like the first generation of Rosenfeld's critics in America, Yiddish scholars writing in the Soviet Union after 1917 used authenticity to validate the literature they promoted. The political constraints imposed on the Soviet Yiddish critics, however, shaped their literary criticism and expression in ways then unknown in America. Although they worked on a host of literary texts, from medieval Yiddish romances, to the works of classic prose writers S. Y. Abramovitch and Sholem Aleykhem, to the modernist poetry of their contemporaries, Marxist-Leninist and, later, Stalinist literary controls limited the type of criticism they could write and the topics on which they could publish. For these critics, origins and authenticity were the keys to their approval or disapproval of a poet; the "Jewish nationalist" strain they perceived in Rosenfeld's poetry was tantamount to treason and greatly diminished the status of the poet in their eyes.

Soviet Yiddish critics focused on two central concerns: tradition and hegemony. Although prerevolutionary Yiddish writers had composed great pieces of literature, their works were not sufficiently "revolutionary." Needing some literature to build upon that would not be considered "bourgeois," many of these critics looked to the American Yiddish Sweatshop poets as the precursors to a new literature.[52] In the decade following the 1917 Revolution, literary controls in the fledgling Soviet state were still relatively liberal. The government, however, by the period of the Cultural Revolution in the late 1920s, had begun to tighten these controls. Government-imposed censorship reached its climax in the mid-1930s, when officials silenced Yiddish literary critics whom they perceived not to be adhering to the Communist Party line.

In March 1918, in the first issue of the first postrevolutionary Yiddish Communist publication, *Di varheyt* (The Truth), A. Agursky, a former Bundist (member of the prerevolutionary Jewish Socialist Party) with past anarchist ties, published an article on Yoysef Bovshover.[53] In this essay, reprinted a few months later as the introduction to a collection of nineteen of Bovshover's poems, one of the very first Yiddish books published in the postrevolutionary period in Russia,[54] Agursky presents the Sweatshop poets as the pioneers of a proletarian poetry he hoped would be perpetuated in the Soviet Union. His critical view, however, would be the minority opinion of Soviet Yiddish critics in the decade following the October Revolution. In February 1926, the Moscow critic Moyshe Litvakov articulated what would be the mainstream position of Soviet Yiddish critics on American Sweatshop poetry into the late 1920s. Published in *Di varheyt*'s new incarnation, *Der emes*, of which Litvakov was editor in chief, "Yerushe un hegemoniye" (Legacy and Hegemony)[55] expresses the two central concerns of Soviet Yiddish critics of this period: "legacy," which denotes the relationship of the Soviet writers to prerevolutionary Yiddish literature; and "hegemony," which denotes the predominance and singular legitimacy of Soviet Yiddish literature over contemporary Yiddish works written in other countries.

On the question of literary legacy, Litvakov writes: "Approaching a cultural legacy in a Marxist manner and uncovering its social origins and meaning, means not to deny it but, on the contrary, it means to fix for it a specific place in the cultural consciousness of the working masses."[56] Litvakov follows the standard Marxist-Leninist opinion concerning the culture of the past: although prerevolutionary culture was indeed not yet proletarian, to build and improve on it, Bolshevik critics in the postrevolutionary period still needed to become intimate with this culture In the case of Soviet Yiddish literature, however, Litvakov argues that it did not benefit from its prerevolutionary works. The October Revolution created a completely new existence for the Jews of the Soviet state, and, as a result, Soviet Yiddish writers were unprepared for life after the revolution; in other words, their literary legacy did not help them. The one area of prerevolutionary literature that Litvakov concedes may have had a limited influence on Soviet Yiddish literature is American Sweatshop poetry. But, even here, his appraisal is ambivalent: "True, our poetry is, in this sense, luckier. It began in the form of Morris Vinchevsky, Morris Rosenfeld, Edelshtat, Bovshover and Avrom Reyzn, all a direct mirroring of the worker's struggle and in close connection with it. However, with the exceptions of Morris Rosenfeld and Avrom Reyzn, it was more of a contrived than an organic poetry."[57]

That said, Litvakov concludes: "In hindsight this inherited legacy was not able to ease our task. Therefore, Soviet Yiddish literature truly felt 'on the brink of a beginning.' "[58] Thus he argues that the Sweatshop poets are more important in a historical sense than in an aesthetic one. Litvakov echoes those American critics who situated Rosenfeld within the "pioneer-classic" scheme, in which they relegate the poet to the former, aesthetically inferior category.

During the Cultural Revolution, which accompanied the first Five Year Plan (1928–32), an economic program of rapid industrialization, urbanization, and forced collectivization of the largely rural Soviet population, Litvakov came under attack for his negative appraisal of the Sweatshop poets. In its vast scope of sweeping change, this movement called for a break with the past and engendered many extreme ideas. One chief manifestation of this trend in

Soviet Yiddish literary criticism was the call for a complete reevaluation and overhaul of the preexisting canon of Yiddish literature. In this search for a new aesthetic, the Sweatshop poets were among the only prerevolutionary writers whose work was deemed worthy of preservation and perpetuation. A chief proponent of this drive was Avrom Vevyorke who, as part of his ideological program, attempted to elevate these writers, as well as the prolific and popular nineteenth-century Yiddish novelist Shomer (N. M. Shaykevitsh), to the status of a "classic" author.

In April 1927, Vevyorke published his first pronouncement on this subject.[59] "Off with the Petit Bourgeois Ban" complains that the canon of Yiddish literature had previously been determined by petit bourgeois tastes, and that a new canon needs to be created, one that would include the works of the neglected authors Vinchevsky, Bovshover, Edelshtat, as well as some by Reyzn and Rosenfeld. He writes: "If Yiddish prose already had giants such as Mendele, Peretz, and Sholem Aleykhem, Yiddish poetry had only the weak attempts of Peretz and, to some extent, Frug's poems. The remaining poems which were written in Yiddish were *badkhones*."[60] In suggesting a new pantheon of venerated writers, Vevyorke asserts that the American Sweatshop poets had enormous social influence and were greatly popular among the mass readership. Furthermore, he contends that these writers introduced important new terms into Yiddish poetry, words such as "*Marx, Engels, barikade* (barricade), *kamf* (struggle), *revolutsyon* (revolution), *Parize komune* (Paris Commune) and *proletariat* (proletariat)."[61] They also integrated European forms into Yiddish poetry, advancing this field beyond *badkhones*. Most important for the critics, however, these poets were real workers who turned to writing, not bourgeois intellectuals who did not care about the masses.

Vevyorke goes on to criticize "our official literary-scholarly institutions," which have been "hypnotized" by the "petit bourgeois aesthetic."[62] He complains that Soviet Yiddish critics have accepted a literary canon determined in a different time and no longer acceptable. In the last lines of his article, Vevyorke offers his solution to this problem: "Our first task is to free ourselves from the canon, which our petit bourgeois aesthetes established, and create our own, which would be in agreement with, and base itself on, the proletarian worldview. Our aesthetic scholarship should be one that will aid the birth of a unique proletarian aesthetic. The first step therefore is to rehabilitate, thoroughly illuminate, and research our banned proletarian literature of the past generation."[63]

Vevyorke wrote several articles entitled "Reviziye" (Revision), a term Soviet Yiddish critics often used to recant previous ideas that had become unacceptable as the central government views of literature changed. Vevyorke, however, employed it to indicate a revision of older and, in his opinion, outdated literary tastes. Indeed, *Revision* is also the title of the book in which he argues for the rehabilitation of the Sweatshop poets, as well as of Shomer.[64] Vevyorke argues that, even though Shomer wrote *shund* (popular, "trashy" works), he nonetheless appealed to a large segment of the Yiddish masses; therefore, on the basis of the demographics of his readership, he must be considered a pioneer of the proletarian aesthetic.

In his second article to appear under the title "Revision," Vevyorke makes the following pronouncements: "If Yiddish prose has its classic writers in Mendele, Peretz, and Sholem Aleykhem, then Yiddish poetry has its classic writers in Vinchevsky, Bovshover, Edelshtat, Morris Rosenfeld and others. These writers were, in their own era, the only modern poets and in certain respects much more original and unique that the classic writers of prose."[65] Unfortunately, Vevyorke offers no evidence to support his grand, canon-defying pronouncements, and his work became the target of sustained attacks, the most comprehensive and intelligent of which was articulated by the Soviet Yiddish critic Meyer Viner.

Viner's polemic focuses on Vevyorke's attempt to rehabilitate Shomer. In "On the Problem of Literary Legacy,"[66] Viner supports the Marxist-Leninist belief that Soviet scholars should not reject past cultural achievements, but rather master them so that they may build upon their accomplishments. Although he agrees that one of the crucial tasks of the Soviet Yiddish critics is to reevaluate "bourgeois" canons, Viner calls Vevyorke's approach simplistic and crude, asserting that the fact of a mass audience does not alone establish an author as a pre-proletarian writer.

Although he concentrates on the critic's view of Shomer, it is clear that Viner objects to Vevyorke's general argument. On "Revision," Viner writes: "A. Vevyorke, even in the chapter of the book which deals with 'Undzer yikhes' [Our Pedigree], allows for a large amount of serious anti-Marxist mistakes which significantly diminish and cripple, in a politically destructive manner, the worth of even the section 'Revision.' "[67] The chapter "Our Pedigree," on which Viner focuses, is the one where Vevyorke deals with Sweatshop poetry.[68]

The intellectual battles that took place among Soviet Yiddish critics reached their climax during the era of the Cultural Revolution. An important element of the Cultural Revolution was the revising of all levels of school curricula, from elementary to postsecondary academies. A central, educational tool for the Soviets was the *khrestomatiya*, a type of literary anthology that served as a classroom reader. With the changes in curricula, there were demands for new materials. In the Soviet Union, where literature was held as one of the chief disseminators of culture, the *khrestomatiyea* was of crucial importance. Therefore, in 1931, the government "Central Peoples' Press" launched a new series of textbooks entitled "Literature for the School." The editors of this series were not satisfied with the previously published *khrestomatii* and so set out to publish new anthologies that would be consistent with the goals of the Cultural Revolution.

The first book in this series was, significantly, a collection of Sweatshop poetry edited by the Soviet Yiddish writer Dovid Kurland. In his introduction to *The First Yiddish Worker-Poets (Morris Vinchevsky, Morris Rosenfeld, Dovid Edelshtat, Yoysef Bovshover),*[69] Kurland minimizes the political transgressions of the poets, explaining that these writers were adversely influenced by their time and place. With the exception of Rosenfeld, whom he brands a "petit bourgeois nationalist," but whose Sweatshop poems are still included in the volume because of their independent worth, Kurland manages the difficult task of painting a positive picture of the other three Sweatshop poets while, at the same time, enumerating their supposed political deviations. He argues that these men are the pioneers of Yiddish proletarian poetry "and the literary legacy that they left us is certainly included as a component of the proletarian literature that we create now in the conditions of the dictatorship of the proletariat, social building, and Cultural Revolution."[70] Kurland establishes the Sweatshop poets as a crucial element of Soviet Yiddish literature without the hyperbole typical of critics such as Vevyorke.

By 1931, the momentum of the Cultural Revolution and its espousal of the Sweatshop poets had become so powerful as to force Moyshe Litvakov—one of the most politically powerful of the interwar Soviet Yiddish critics—to revise his earlier position. In an article he published that year, Litvakov recants his earlier attack on Sweatshop poetry: "I must make clear here that the statement 'more of a contrived than an organic' is, in this regard, incorrect. I must also say that this same expression in my later articles on this same subject is in fact rescinded, and if I should indeed be considered guilty of something, it is in the fact that, in rescinding it, I did not emphasize that I was rescinding it."[71] There is little doubt that the critic composed this convoluted and banal revision of his earlier beliefs in response to the pressures and forces of the Cultural Revolution. The fact that Litvakov—still editor in chief of *Der emes*—believed it necessary to revise his earlier opinions, testifies to the power and influence of this movement in the arena of Yiddish literature in the Soviet Union.

The Cultural Revolution came to an abrupt end in 1932, however. The Soviet government decided that this policy of radical change, especially in the fields of literature and education, was destructive, and thus began the era of "The Great Retreat," a term coined by the historian Nicholas Timasheff, who used it as title for his 1946 book.[72] The radicalism of the Cultural Revolution was abandoned and culture became tightly institutionalized and controlled. Radical curricula in schools and universities were scrapped, traditional plans of study were reinstated, and the government increased its control over the output of literature.

Because critics could no longer minimize the "petit bourgeois" political affiliations of the Sweatshop poets, Soviet Yiddish appraisal of Sweatshop poetry reached its nadir during this period. Rosenfeld's "nationalistic" and "Zionistic" tendencies, which had already disqualified him from most discussions of Sweatshop poetry, now branded him as an official persona non grata among Soviet Yiddish scholars. Vinchevsky, who had been dubbed "Der zeyde" (the Grandfather) of Yiddish proletarian literature,[73] was now denounced for his involvement in the Bund and for his own "nationalistic" poetry. In the wake the antigovernment activities and demonstrations conducted by anarchist groups in Spain against that country's pro-Soviet government, however, the worst crime of all for the Soviet Yiddish critics in the early to mid-1930s was anarchism. For Soviet Yiddish literature, this meant that the political affiliations of Bovshover and Edelshtat could no longer be swept under the rug; they needed to be directly addressed.[74]

One notable exception to this reactionary appraisal of Sweatshop poetry was written by the Yiddish literary scholar Kalman Marmor, author of numerous articles on Rosenfeld. A strong proponent of Rosenfeld's works, a close friend of the poet's, and a Communist sympathizer who visited Kiev in 1935, Marmor headed up the redaction of a planned three-volume collection of Sweatshop poetry, of which only the first two volumes were published. In an essay Marmor published while in Kiev—an obvious attempt to rehabilitate Rosenfeld in the Soviet Union, which proved to be too little too late—he admits the poet's transgressions, but attempts to offset them with praise for satiric poems that Marmor culled mostly from manuscripts composed by Rosenfeld around 1917, six years before his death. As I noted in the previous chapter, these works are satiric treatments of the Yiddish press in America, especially of the *Forverts* and its longtime editor Abraham Cahan. Although Marmor understands that Rosenfeld's involvement with anarchist and Zionist parties was problematic for the Soviets, he uses Marxist-Leninist reasoning to argue that Rosenfeld, as a product of his environment, could not have acted otherwise. Moreover, the poet was simply experimenting with national motifs in Rosenfeld's Zionist poems which do not represent a sustained phase in his writing, and, which, in any event, are redeemed by Rosenfeld's proletarian and satiric poems. By stressing that the satiric poems were written late in Rosenfeld's life and that they are aimed against the "bourgeois" press in America, Marmor seems to imply that Rosenfeld recanted in his last years and rededicated himself to the masses.

The battle over Rosenfeld among Soviet Yiddish critics highlights the tension between "high" and "low" Marxism. The high Marxist model, based on the writings of Marx and Engels and then later interpreted and elaborated on mainly by Lenin and Plekhanov, supports the value of pre-Marxist literature. In the case of Yiddish, this meant that critics such as Meyer Viner and Max Erik held that prerevolutionary Yiddish writers, in particular, S. Y. Abramovitch and Sholem Aleykhem, despite their own shortcoming as bourgeois members of Jewish society, still offer an important and valuable understanding of the Jewish masses and their works when interpreted through a Marxist lens. These principles oppose the more simplistic and superficial criteria of the proponents of the low model who seize upon certain external aspects of literature—in the case of Vevyorke's article on Shomer, the intended mass reading audience—in order to support their assertions that this literature deserved to be part of the proletarian canon. Indeed, it was these very same low or "vulgar" Marxist ideals which dominated the Soviet Yiddish arm of the Cultural Revolution and which quickly fell out of fashion as soon as the political environment changed and the central government imposed tightened control over the fields of literature and literary criticism.

Although Rosenfeld was vilified among Soviet Yiddish critics, this politically tendentious understanding of the poet had limited influence on the formation of the canon of Yiddish literature. The most lasting opinion of the poet, one that, in essence, excluded him from the canon, was the promodernist appraisal of Di yunge. Before, and certainly after, the Second World War, Yiddish literary study was centered in America. With three full generations of poets to consider, American Yiddish scholars set about determining a canon for this relatively young field of poetry. Influenced both by the opinions of Di yunge and by the modernist demands of New Criticism, the anthologists of American Yiddish poetry marginalized Rosenfeld in their respective canons. At best, Rosenfeld was treated as a pioneer whose works, though of little aesthetic value, still held historical importance; at worst, the Sweatshop poet's accomplishments were completely ignored.

The only anthologies, whether in Yiddish or in English, that contain more than one or two poems by Rosenfeld are historical in their presentation of Yiddish poetry. The first of these is the *American Yiddish Poetry Anthology*,[75] edited by Moyshe Basin, a poet associated with Di yunge. In his introduction, Basin asserts that the chief significance of "pioneer" poets such as Rosenfeld, Yehoyesh

(Shloyme Blumgortn), and Avrom Reyzn is that they "prepared the foundation . . ." [76] Basin presents Rosenfeld first in his anthology, offering readers twenty-nine poems that span the poet's career, and that represent the various genres in which he wrote,: the Sweatshop, national, satirical, and lyrical. [77]

A similar historical approach, which makes certain concessions to the aesthetic, is evident in *A Treasury of Yiddish Poetry*, coedited by the Yiddish critic and poet Eliezer Greenberg and the American literary scholar Irving Howe. [78] Here, too, Rosenfeld is placed within the first generation of "pioneers" of Yiddish poetry, but it is clear that the poet's role is one of historical progenitor, and that true poetry begins only after him. In their introduction, the editors spend far more time discussing Di yunge than Rosenfeld's generation of Yiddish poets; they offer only a few of Rosenfeld's poems by way of introducing a historical survey of Yiddish poetry.

The most influential of the promodernist anthologies is the bilingual *Penguin Book of Modern Yiddish Verse*, also coedited by Howe together with noted scholars Ruth Wisse and Khone Shmeruk, published by a highly respected press known for its collections of canonical literature. [79] In this more "modern" and "poetic" anthology, older poets such as Yehoyesh and Rosenfeld are hardly represented at all. [80] As Ruth Wisse states, the goal of the editors was to create a collection of modern texts that would be accompanied by "new" texts, intended not as literal translations of the original works, but rather as somewhat re-created versions of the Yiddish poems that would be highly readable English language works: "We invited English-language poets to create an English poem for every Yiddish original. Where necessary, we supplied the translators with the kind of apparatus provided by The Poem Itself, but through what we hoped was clever matchmaking between the Yiddish poet and the English-language poet most likely to love him, we tried to inspire the birth of a new generation of poems." [81] Although, not surprisingly, the literal meanings of the poems are often sacrificed, the overall quality of this anthology is excellent. Several poets, such as Mani Leyb, Moyshe-Leyb Halpern, Itsik Manger, and Avrom Sutzkever, receive more attention than others, a natural consequence that, in all anthologies, reflects the tastes of the editors. It is therefore in the very selection of which poets shall live and which shall die, to paraphrase Wisse, that a clear modernist aesthetic determines the content of this book, and presents only certain pre-Di yunge poets such as Yoysef Rolnik and Avrom Reyzn—older poets whom several of Di yunge celebrated as sympathetic to and aligned with their own goals—in a relatively extensive manner, while offering readers only one poem by Rosenfeld and none at all by his contemporary Sweatshop poets.

Benjamin and Barbara Harshav express a more pronounced promodernist bias in their *American Yiddish Poetry*.[82] This large and beautifully illustrated bilingual anthology presents a selection of American Yiddish poets with broad samples that span their respective careers, demonstrating the editors' full understanding of the aesthetics and historical circumstances of these writers. Despite its title, however, the anthology is not a comprehensive survey but rather a presentation of seven modernist artists, many of whom are associated with the high modernist literary group In zikh.

Although critics of Yiddish literature vary in their choice of Rosenfeld's works and modes, almost all label him a "proletarian poet" and invest the bulk of their analytic energies on his Sweatshop poems. Some, especially American and Yiddishist critics, chose authenticity as their main evaluational criterion. For them, the more authentic and true to the poet's life experiences his poems are, the more literary value they possess. On the other hand, under tremendous governmental pressure to perpetuate a Marxist-Leninist and, later, Stalinist canon of modern Yiddish literature, the Soviet Yiddish critics could not divide the poet's works from his life. Even the members of Di yunge with their motto of "art for art's sake" could not divorce Rosenfeld's poetry from his personal life, arguing that his works were completely permeated by his political views. It is only with the next generation of American Yiddish writers, the high modernists of In zikh, that Rosenfeld receives a more balanced treatment. Despite all attempts at rehabilitation, however, the anti-Rosenfeld biases of Di yunge persisted in defining the canon of modern Yiddish poetry.

Though indeed a pioneer Yiddish poetry, Rosenfeld created some of the most lasting works in Yiddish literature. He began his career composing propagandistic poems within the narrow confines of nineteenth-century Yiddish poetry, but quickly expanded his scope. In his mature proletarian or Sweatshop poems—which stand out as his best—Rosenfeld expresses the collective suffering of the Eastern European working masses. With scant Yiddish poetic tradition to draw upon, Rosenfeld took common themes, language, and poetic forms and employed them in uncommon ways that transcended linguistic borders and earned his works international appeal.

3

The Melodramatic and Sentimental Sweatshop

Many critics of Yiddish literature consider Morris Rosenfeld one of four chief representatives of the first generation of Yiddish writers in America. The Sweatshop poets of this generation—including Yoysef Bovshover, Dovid Edelshtat, and Morris Vinchevsky—protested the working conditions of their immigrant laborer readers and called on them to revolt against the capitalist system. To attract the attention of the large, semieducated, working-class readership they sought to inspire, the Sweatshop poets appropriated a poetic model that poets of the *haskala*—their immediate predecessors—had employed, and one I shall term the "exhortative poem." Later, in his mature Sweatshop poetry, Rosenfeld expands the scope of this model within the context of his sentimental and melodramatic thematics.

By the turn of the twentieth century, Rosenfeld lost interest in the strictly exhortative poem and the hollow, unconvincing messages of hope and revolution it promoted, turning from a propagandistic poet to an existential one. He saw no solutions to the dreariness of immigrant shop life forthcoming, and he no longer believed that any voluntary, willful action by his worker readers could change their situation. Therefore, Rosenfeld chose a more suitable vehicle for his pessimism, namely, the sentimental-melodramatic mode that shaped poetry on thematic, semantic, and formal levels.

The exhortative poem finds its first sustained, modern expression in late-eighteenth-century poetry, particularly in the English literature of sensibility and in the German literature of Sturm und Drang. Although these literary trends found a receptive audience among the early—and mid-nineteenth-century *haskala* writers, the exhortative poem did not come to the fore in Hebrew and Yiddish poetry until the final decades of the nineteenth century. As enthusiasm for Jewish Enlightenment ideals waned, many writers began to embrace new political principles and to express these in their poetry. The writers of late *haskala* poetry employed the exhortative poem, but the form found its most sustained expression in the Hebrew Hibbat Zion (Love of Zion) school, and in the works of the Yiddish Sweatshop poets.

The exhortative poem possesses a number of specific traits, most notably, it contains no narrative plot, but rather follows the development of an idea that is expressed in simple terms and repeated or illustrated in several forms. It also establishes a clearly designated relationship between a speaker—an impersonal, yet empathetic "I" who propounds ideas, often pointing to the "truth"—and the speaker's audience, a collective "you." In the Hebrew and Yiddish exhortative poem, that audience is often the Jewish people, the workers of the world, or Jewish workers. The speaker's need to convince and, indeed, to motivate his audience creates a strong rhetorical tone, and the poet relies heavily on sentiment to promote the main ideas of his works.

When the first generation of American Yiddish poets began their careers in the 1880s, most turned to the exhortative poem to express their political beliefs. Whereas *haskala* writers had called on their readers to shed the trappings of traditional Jewish life and to embrace secular European culture and education, Sweatshop poets, responding to what they perceived as the new, more pragmatic priorities of their immigrant, working-class audience, gave the exhortative poem a new, more urgent message. Specifically, Rosenfeld and his contemporaries invested the exhortative poem with their preferred ideologies, namely, socialism, communism, and anarchism.[1] These poets demanded a new, class-based consciousness from their readers; they used the exhortative poem to present the "folk" with a new, politically charged message that demanded nothing less than a workers' revolution.

Rosenfeld, in his mature Sweatshop poetry, expanded—and often subverted—the model of the exhortative poem, using the language and motifs of melodrama and sentimentalism to convey the despair and pessimism that pervade his works. Although the poet was all too willing to shed the metaphoric, linguistic, and generic conventions of the exhortative model, he refused to interfere with its prosody. Indeed, ever mindful of the crucial need to communicate with his readers, Rosenfeld would tighten his grip on exhortative prosody in his mature Sweatshop poems, using it to cultivate the symbiotic relationship with his readers so vital to the meaning of his poetry—and that of all melodramatic-sentimental literature.

Regulated prosody is crucial to the exhortative poem for several reasons. Because the main point of the exhortative poem is to communicate a central idea to its audience, the poem must be memorable; the speaker is lecturing and needs to speak forcefully. Nineteenth-century Hebrew and Yiddish poets often relied on consistent, emphatic prosody to catch and hold the attention of their readers. Furthermore, the formal poetic (prosodic) features—most notably, meter, rhythm, and rhyme—of this otherwise propagandistic and often "unpoetic" model needed to be emphasized to highlight the poetic nature of the discourse. Finally, with the speaker an abstract, impersonal entity (the "good man") addressing a collective entity (the working class), there is little room within the speaker's crucial and practical message for individual deviation from prosodic norms. In the exhortative model, because the poem expresses collective ideas, the prosody must be fixed: it should not express one-time, idiosyncratic *shtimung* (feeling). Whenever great commercial or industrial development has produced a mass proletariat, notes literary scholar M. H. Abrams, "the attempt to translate Scriptural prophecy into revolutionary action has been a recurrent phenomenon."[2] Exhortative poetry is largely motivated by the idea of "the belief in an imminent revolution, of which the effect on the well-being of humanity will be sudden, absolute, and universal"[3] and embodies the following six attitudes: (1) the revolution will, by an inescapable and cleansing explosion of violence and destruction, reconstitute the existing political, social, and moral order absolutely, from its very foundations, and so (2) bring about abruptly, or in a remarkably short time, the shift from the present era of profound evil, suffering, and disorder to an era of peace, justice, and optimal conditions for general happiness; (3) it will be led by a militant élite, who will find ranged against them the forces dedicated to preserving the present evils, consolidated in a specific institution or class or race; (4) though it will originate in a particular and critical time and place, it will, through irresistible contagion, spread everywhere, to include all humanity; (5) its benefits will endure for a very long time, perhaps forever, because the transformation of the our institutional circumstances and cultural ambience will heal the intellectual and spiritual malaise that has brought us to our present plight; and (6) it is inevitable because it is guaranteed either by an immanent something, not ourselves, which makes for the ineluctable triumph of total justice, community, and happiness on earth.[4]

These ideas, motivated largely by "fervent eschatological expectations,"[5] came to dominate Yiddish poetry in the 1880s and 1890s when the newly arrived and arriving Eastern European Jewish immigrants took their place at the bottom of the American economic system.

Morris Vinchevsky began his long and multilingual career in the 1870s as a Hebrew poet and journalist, often writing under the pseudonyms "Ben nets" (Son of a Hawk) and "Yig'al ish haruakh" (Yig'al the Man of Spirit). Vinchevsky is credited as the "father"—and, by Soviet Yiddish critics in the 1930s, the "grandfather"—of Communist Yiddish literature. When Rosenfeld published his first poems at the end of 1886, Vinchevsky had already begun to compose poetry in Yiddish and was the dominant figure in the infant genre of Sweatshop poetry. The younger Edelshtat and Bovshover, who began their careers several years later, produced relatively little. Edelshtat published his first poem in 1889, but his career was cut short by his premature death in 1892, at the age of 26. Bovshover, who began publishing in 1890, ceased writing in 1899 when he was hospitalized for mental illness. The works of these early Sweatshop poets resonated with a newly proletarianized immigrant audience; many of the poems were recited at political demonstrations. Indeed, immigrant workers in the shops often sang the most popular of these works, which had been set to music.[6] The poetic speakers in these poems respond to the new, industrialized condition of the Jewish working class and, assuming a leadership position, attempt to convince readers that their message is important, just, and inevitable.

In "A gezang tsum folk" (A Song to the People), Bovshover's poetic speaker implores the working masses to examine the world anew and realize that they are being exploited by the upper classes. Although he paints a pessimistic image of the present, the speaker does not allow the unjust system to overwhelm him and, in the poem's final stanza, he instructs his audience:

Heyb uf dayne oygn, o folk, gey aroys fun di finstere kvorim,
heyb uf dayne oygn tsu mizrekh un mayrev, tsu tsofn un dorem,
un nem di geyarshente oytsres un nem fun dayn arbet di peyres,
un shafendik leb un genisndik shaf in di frayere deyres.[7]

[Raise your eyes, O people, emerge from your dark graves,
raise your eyes toward the east and west, toward the north
    and south,
and take your inherited treasures and take the fruits of your labor,
and live productively and produce enjoyably in the freer
generations.]

"A Song to the People," like most Sweatshop poems, concludes on a hope-filled note. With a naïveté that pervades Yiddish proletarian poetry, the speaker appeals to a general sense of morality by pronouncing his inherent belief that the physical products of manual labor—its "treasures" and "fruits"—rightly belong to the workers who produced them.

In this final stanza, although both pairs of rhymes *(kvorim-dorem* and *peyres-deyres)* make use of the infrequently occurring Hebrew element in Yiddish, it is the first pair that is especially significant. Whereas the two words of the second pair are linked both grammatically, being the plural forms of the nouns *peyre* (fruit) and *dor* (generation) and, at least in a loose sense, semantically, as engendered living things, those of the first pair, *kvorim* (graves) and *dorem* (south), are connected neither grammatically nor semantically, providing readers with an unexpected and interesting rhyme.

Although Sweatshop poetry is criticized for its repetitiveness and adherence to traditional poetic forms, this rigidity often produces interesting results. Consider another example of a classic Sweatshop poem, Dovid Edelshtat's "In kamf" (In Struggle), which begins:

Mir vern gehast un getribn,
mir vern geplogt un farfolgt,
un ales derfar vayl mir libn
dos oreme shmakhtende folk.

Mir vern ershosn, gehangen,
men baroybt undz dos lebn un rekht
derfar vayl mir emes farlangen
un frayheyt far oreme knekht![8]

[We are hated and chased,
we are harassed and persecuted,
and all because we love
the poor languishing people.

We are shot, hanged,
our lives and rights are stolen from us
because we desire truth
and freedom for poor slaves.]

"In Struggle" demonstrates how the form of a poem can be employed to emphasize its meaning. Edelshtat uses anaphora, a rhetorical device common in Sweatshop poetry, in which the same word or phrase is repeated in successive lines, here to highlight the blight of the workers' vanguard "we," with whom the poet identifies. He builds tension by repeating "mir vern" (we are, we become), adding to it the acts of the upper class against the leaders of the workers' revolution, progressively heightening the action: in the first stanza they are persecuted; in the second, murdered. He further emphasizes this tension with his use of metric regularity, which pounds out the rhythm of the poem. The poem paints an increasingly pessimistic portrait of the current situation, yet ends on an optimistic note, in this case, an ominous warning to the oppressors:

Ir kent undz ermordn, tiranen!
Naye kemfer vet brengn di tsayt—
un mir kemfn, mir kemfn biz vanen
di gantse velt vet vern bafrayt.[9]

[You can murder us, tyrants!
New fighters will bring about the time—
and we'll fight, we'll fight until
the whole world will be free.]

The final stanza of almost all early Sweatshop poems provides an upbeat climax. Because the radical Yiddish press aimed to agitate its readers to action, most of the poetry in this genre concludes with a positive, prophetic vision of the future and the life awaiting the shop worker after the revolution. For example, Morris Vinchevsky's "Di tsukunft" (The Future) concludes:

Mutik brider, mutik shvester!
Ot der kamf, der letster, grester,
ruft aykh fun di tukhle nester
afn frayen feld;
alzo, mutik in di rayen,
in di rayen, tsu bafrayen,
tsu bafrayen un banayen,
undzer alte velt![10]

[Be brave brothers, be brave sisters!
The battle, the final one, the greatest one,
calls you from your moldy nests
to the free field;
therefore, be brave in the lines,
in the lines, to free,
to free and rebuild,
our old world!]

In addressing the situation of the workers, Vinchevsky has his speaker employ the metaphor of war to intensify the emotional appeal of his poem, as do other Sweatshop poets that of theirs. His use of sentimental language, likening the workers to family members—"brothers" and "sisters"—and of incremental repetition further strengthens this appeal. Skillfully manipulating the stock language of Yiddish poetry, drawn from European literature, Vinchevsky creates a satisfying momentum and tension within his poem and endows it with a richness of internal rhyme.

Although, like many of his poems, "The Future" is a call to arms, Vinchevsky also wrote several works that conclude on a more pessimistic note. In poems such as "Dos ufele in vald" (The Baby in the Forest), "Shtum, toyb, blind" (Dumb, Deaf, Blind), and one of his best-known creations, "Dray shvester" (Three Sisters), set in London, where the poet himself lived for several years, he experiments with rudimentary forms of melodrama:

> Di yingste farkoyft dortn blumen,
> di mitlste—bendlekh fun shikh,
> un shpet in der nakht zet men kumen
> di eltste, vos handlt mit zikh.[11]

> [There the youngest one sells flowers,
> the middle one—shoelaces,
> and late at night you can see coming
> the oldest one, who sells herself.]

Instead of a discourse on an abstract or ideological experience, Vinchevsky focuses here on a particular and individualized group of people. He employs a trope common to the melodramatic mode: innocence and virtue destroyed:

> Dokh shpet ba der nakht, ven zey kumen
> tsum nest, vos zey rufn "a heym,"
> banetsn zey bendlekh un blumen
> mit trern, vos flisn geheym.[12]

[But late at night when they come
to the nest they call "a home,"
they soak laces and flowers
with tears that flow in secret.]

In contrast to most Sweatshop poems, however, "Three Sisters" does not end with the victory of virtue restored. Instead, the poem ends in tears, a common trope of melodramatic literature. Although Vinchevsky uses the trope to represent sadness, he extends it to include both shameful and harmful elements. The sisters do not cry while they work; they weep in private. Customers would not want to purchase flowers, shoelaces, or sex from despondent girls. Yet, when they finally express their sorrow within the privacy of their home, their tears still have a destructive effect, saturating and, presumably, ruining the merchandise that provides their livelihood.

Although Vinchevsky was one of the first Yiddish poets to include melodrama and sentimentalism in his poetry, these elements do not find sustained expression in his works. It is Rosenfeld who fully incorporates them into his own poetry, thereby creating a new and original aesthetic in Yiddish literature: still writing in the call-to-arms vein, he recasts the Sweatshop poem and endows it with a more concrete, existential nature, which dramatizes the suffering of the immigrant worker. The propagandistic works Rosenfeld published in the radical Yiddish press during the 1880s and 1890s represent the first stage of his career, during which his poems are similar in tone and theme to those of his fellow Sweatshop poets. In "Der tsveyfakher may" (The Two-Sided May), the speaker connects the blooming of nature with an impending workers' revolution and concludes this poem with a threat to the upper classes:

Un aykh zog ikh raykhe tiranen,
zeyer noent iz ayer sof!
Der arbets man iz ufgeshtanen

fun zayn tifn langn shlof . . .
Ir megt im oykh di veg fartsamen
ale mitl vendt on,
dokh zog ikh aykh in varheyts nomen,
az zign vet di frayheyts fon![13]

[And I say to you rich tyrants,
your end is very near!
The working man has arisen
from his deep, long sleep . . .
You may block his path,
employ every means,
but I tell you in the name of truth,
that the flag of freedom shall prevail!]

Like many of Rosenfeld's early poems, "The Two-Sided May"
is bombastic in tone and contains much the same figurative language as the poems of his contemporaries. Specifically, the poet
uses tropes that fall into two metaphoric categories common in
Sweatshop poetry: war and crime. Rosenfeld's poetic speakers
continually refer to the upper classes as "royber" (robbers),
"merder" (murderers), and "shvindler" (swindlers), whereas the
workers are called "heldn" (heroes), who engage in "krig" (battle)
on the "shlakhtfeld" (battlefield). The central quest for the protagonists of Sweatshop poetry, however, is that of "varheyt" (truth),
and the speakers of these poems are often concerned with
"tsaygn" (pointing to) this truth. For example, the dead speak to
the protagonists of several poems from beyond the grave, from
"oylem ho'emes" (the World of Truth), where, according to literary tradition, they are afforded a privileged view of the "true" nature of things.

Much of Rosenfeld's early Sweatshop poetry is optimistic in
tone, but there are traces of the despair that will consume his mature works in this genre. For example, some of Rosenfeld's early

poems focus on the suffering of the workers without offering a positive solution for their oppressive existence. The editors of the radical Yiddish press rejected these despondent poems because they lacked the optimistic tone deemed necessary to stir a proletarian audience to social action. Some of these editors even called the poet a "traitor" to their political causes. Thus the only venue for Rosenfeld to publish these poems was his books, most of which were self-financed.

In *Di gloke* (1888), Rosenfeld's first collection, there is a poetic cycle entitled "Lebnsbilder" (Life Portraits)[14] that is not typical of the poet's early works. Here we see the genesis of the melodramatic and sentimental modes that characterize Rosenfeld's later works. "Regs, regs" (Rags, Rags) is a poem in which the title represents the last words of an old ragpicker who dies, neglected in the middle of the street; "Di likht farkoyferin" (The Candle Seller) tells of a homeless widow who fails to attract any customers and at the end of the poem is arrested, along with her child, for vagrancy; and "Gey! Gey!" (Go! Go!), the final poem in this series and one of the first instances in which Rosenfeld employs the poetic "I," presents the case of a husband-father who complains of his punishing and bitter life as a sweatshop worker.

In "Ambelens" (Ambulance), a construction worker is injured on the job. Following the accident, the protagonist is brought to the hospital, where he is met by his grieving family. After the "cold" and "indifferent" doctor—an unsympathetic, upper-class "enemy"—announces that his patient has no more than five minutes to live, the man delivers his final words from his deathbed, a typical melodramatic setting:

> Mayne kinder, o, froy . . .
> Vu bin ikh? Oy . . .
> Ikh shtarb . . . Un ir?!
> Ba der arbet a shteyn . . .

Tsushpaltn dem kop . . . Nit veyn . . .
Der tiran . . . Er . . . Vey iz mir![15]

[My children, oh, wife . . .
Where am I? Oh . . .
I am dying . . . And you?!
At work a stone . . .
Split my head . . . Don't cry . . .
The tyrant . . . He . . . Woe is me!]

In a typical Sweatshop poem, the speaker would seize the moment of his death to pronounce his hope for the future without especial concern for himself or his family. Yet here, in a revolutionary twist, Rosenfeld instead has his injured and dying protagonist not concern himself with the workers' cause, but instead wonder how his family will support itself after his death. In the stanza's final line, a crucial place Sweatshop poets reserve for hope-filled pronouncements about the future, the speaker begins by calling his boss, whom he holds responsible for his death, "the tyrant," but loses his ideological focus and can only emit a clichéd expression of personal sorrow, "vey iz mir" (woe is me). Far from the typical speech of the Sweatshop hero who promises revenge and a better future for the working class, the dying man's comments are the human and barely coherent final words of manual laborer fatally injured on the job.

In this and other poems of the "Life Portraits" cycle, Rosenfeld relates to the existential condition of his characters. Which highlights one of the crucial differences of his mature Sweatshop poems, whose concrete descriptions of characters and situations and whose depressed and pessimistic tone contrast sharply with Rosenfeld's earlier, politically motivated poems, which are abstract, propagandistic, and, for the most part, optimistic. This decisive shift in tone and thematics is largely the result of Rosenfeld's incorporating the melodrama and sentimentalism into his later poems.

In *Tragedy and Melodrama*, Robert Heilman describes the central difference between these two literary modes as a function of the agency of the protagonist. The tragic hero is an active character who is torn, self-divided, and, as such, his own worst enemy, whereas the melodramatic hero is essentially a passive character who, existing in "the gloomy world," to use a term Heilman borrows from John Webster's *The Duchess of Malfi*, is acted upon by the outside forces of disaster:

> What is done to me, what is too much for me—that is the heart of the gloomy world. The plays of the gloomy world deal largely with shadows and darkness imposed rather than chosen. This is the realm of disaster—the desolation of life when the sea or other forces of nature find their victims; the death and suffering of those who are the victims of societal power, political ruthlessness, or war; the disintegration of those who cannot cope with the exigencies of the life in which they find themselves, the sad maneuvers of victims of disillusionment, the beating down of those who get in the way of evil men.[16]

In melodrama, the protagonist is not divided against himself; he is a "good guy" who suffers from the evil acts of "bad guys."

However trivial or simpleminded melodrama may seem on its surface, Heilman explains that it is at its core "a stable central structure that appears in all times and in trivial and sober plays alike"; he calls it "one of the persistent fundamental structures of literature" that "draws upon permanent human attitudes."[17] In the classic battle between good and evil, good is personified in the protagonist, who is confronted and overwhelmed by the external threat of evil. Although Heilman develops these features of melodramatic conflict in the context of drama, they translate easily to modern Yiddish poetry. In almost all Sweatshop poems, the melodramatic conflict is clear: the workers are the good, innocent victims of the evil capitalist system, which is personified by the bosses. In his mature works, Rosenfeld develops this conflict within his own "gloomy world," the sweatshop, which, in the poet's oeuvre, is a microcosm for the life of the immigrant laborer.

"In tragedy," Heilman goes on to say, "the conflict is within man; in melodrama, it is between men, or between men and things. Tragedy is concerned with the nature of man, melodrama with the habits of men and things. A habit normally reflects part of a nature [but i]n melodrama we accept the part for the whole; this is a convention of the form."[18] The protagonist of melodrama "is essentially 'whole' [which] implies neither greatness nor moral perfection, but rather an absence of the basic inner conflict."[19] This melodramatic singularity of outlook and emotion Heilman terms "monopathy." In Rosenfeld, it takes the form of despair, and the habit that represents the entire nature is labor. In other words, for his protagonists, life in the sweatshop sets the tenor of their entire lives. This situation is most evident in the longer of his two poems, entitled "Di svet shap" (The Sweatshop):

Es royshn in shap azoy vild di mashinen,
az oftmol farges ikh in roysh dos ikh bin;
ikh ver in dem shreklekhn tuml farlorn,
mayn ikh vert dort botl, ikh ver a mashin:
Ikh arbet un arbet, un arbet on kheshbn,
es shaft zikh, un shaft zikh, un shaft zikh on tsol:
Far vos? Un far vemen? Ikh veys nit, ikh freg nit,
vi kumt a mashine tsu denken a mol?[20]
[The machines in the shop roar so wildly,
that often I forget that I exist in the noise;
I get lost in the horrible din,
my "I" is destroyed, I become a machine:

I work and work and work with no accounting,
it produces and produces and produces without end:
Why? And for whom? I do not know, I do not ask,
how would a machine know how to think?]

This poem, one of Rosenfeld's finest, represents his first effort at complete focusing on the inner life of the speaker within the all-encompassing confines of the sweatshop. In the first stanza, the speaker declares that the manual labor he performs threatens his existence. The death motif appears abundantly in Rosenfeld's earlier works and the works of other contemporary poets, but it appears in a strictly literal sense: the workers who die do so as a result of fatal accidents at the workplace. In "The Sweatshop," on the other hand, the speaker does not die literally. Rather, his "I" does, namely, his individuality, as he slowly becomes a machine. Here, for the first time in Yiddish poetry, is an example of metaphorical death as a result of the sweatshop.

Rosenfeld makes artful use of regulated prosody, particularly to mimic the deadly repetitiveness of mechanized labor, to complement the thematic elements of this poem. Whereas the iamb (two syllables—unstressed, stressed) is the predominant metric foot in most of his poems, he uses the amphibrach (three syllables—unstressed, stressed, unstressed) in "The Sweatshop." The deadeningly repetitive prosody and rhyme scheme (ABCB-DEFE) of the eight-line stanzas reinforce the literally and metaphorically murderous power of mechanical labor in a non-stop flow.

Rosenfeld's use of repetitive language only intensifies this feeling. In the first stanza, the verbs *arbetn* (to work) and *shafn zikh* (to produce) are repeated in the first person, "Ikh arbet un arbet, un arbet" (I work and work, and work) and in the third person, "Es shaft zikh, un shaft zikh, un shaft zikh" (It produces, and produces and produces). Not only does this repetition mimic the repetitive nature of the labor, but by shifting from first to third person, Rosenfeld also points to the dehumanization of the speaker-worker as he is transformed into an automaton, thereby underlining the metaphorically deadening effect of manual labor.

Unlike Rosenfeld's earlier works, the entire drama of "The Sweatshop" takes place in the speaker's mind as he reacts to the overwhelming sights and sounds of his workplace, particularly those of the double-faced clock. On a literal level, the clock is a relentless marker of the steady passing of time, controlling the work day by signaling, with its whistle, when the workers are to break and when they are to resume their labor:

Der zeyger in vorkshap, er rut nit afile,
er vayzt alts un klapt alts un vekt nokhanand;
gezogt hot a mentsh mir amol di badaytung:
zayn vayzn un vekn, dort ligt a farshtand. (9)

[The clock in the workshop does not even rest,
it keeps showing and ticking and waking continuously;
once, someone told me its meaning:
in its showing and waking, there lies an understanding.]

After the speaker states his practical understanding of the clock's function, he pauses to reflect on a distant memory of a possibly deeper meaning of the clock:

Nor etvos gedenkt zikh mir, punkt vi fun kholem;
der zeyger, er vekt in mir lebn un zin,
un nokh epes, ikh hob fargesn, nit freg es!
Ikh veys nit, ikh veys nit, ikh bin a mashin! (9)

[But I remember something, just like in a dream,
the clock awakens in me life and sense,

and something else, I forgot, do not ask!
I do not know, I do not know, I am a machine!]

Try as he might, the speaker cannot grasp the clock's second meaning, strongly hinted by the "life and sense" it awakens in him. By briefly reclaiming thought and life—two human qualities expropriated by the sweatshop—the second, deeper meaning of the clock threatens to disrupt the monotonous mechanical dehumanization of the speaker. Unfortunately, memory is no match for the sweatshop's dehumanization, which has brought about his metaphoric demise.

In the following stanza, the speaker delves deeper into his thoughts, hearing in the ticking of the clock the voice of the oppressive boss:

Un tsaytnvayz ven ikh derher shoyn dem zeyger,
farshtey ikh gants andersh zayn vayzn, zayn shprakh;
mir dakht, az es nuket mikh dortn der un-ru,
kh'zol arbetn, arbetn, merer, a sakh!
Ikh her in zayn ton nor dem bos's vildn beyzer,
zayn finstern kuk in di vayzer di tsvey;
der zeyger, mir skrukhet, mir dakht, az es traybt mikh
un ruft mikh "mashine!" un shrayt tsu mir: "ney!"(9)

[And sometimes when I hear the clock,
I come to a quite different understanding of its pointing, its language;
it seems to me that its restless nature eggs me on,
to work, work, more, a lot!
I hear in its sound only the boss's angry rebuke,
his dark look in its two hands;
the clock, I shudder, it seems to drive me
and call me "machine!" and scream at me, "Sew!"]

The clock drives the speaker, causes him to shudder, even seems to shout at him, yet it is clear that these effects are all products of the speaker's imagination. Unlike the speaker in the earlier exhortative poems of the Sweatshop poets or the *haskala*, he is not sermonizing or lecturing, but expressing his subjective thoughts and feelings as a multidimensional, conscious being.

By focusing on the inner life of the speaker and making his consciousness the site of narrative action, Rosenfeld internalizes the exhortative poem, subverting earlier Sweatshop poetry. The speaker of "The Sweatshop" imbues the shop clock with metaphorical meaning. The never-ending movement of time, as embodied in the clock, represents history, which in Rosenfeld's early works is on the side of the worker. In these early poems, as well as in those of Bovshover, Edelshtat, and Vinchevsky, there is an inherent belief in the eventual and certain victory of the workers over the bosses, a victory guaranteed by inevitable historical processes. The speaker in "The Sweatshop" alludes to this idea, but he acknowledges that it is only a distant memory, which is quickly extinguished because he must focus on his job. Instead of an optimistic view of time, Rosenfeld offers a critique of the Marxist belief so important to Yiddish Sweatshop poetry that manual labor has the power to free one's mind. In "The Sweatshop," the exact opposite is true; here manual labor destroys free thought and transforms the workers into unthinking robots.

Rosenfeld's break with past ideology, however, is not clear-cut. As his speaker in "The Sweatshop" continues to contemplate the clock and build upon its meaning, he invokes a familiar metaphor. The boss leaves the shop for lunch, the workers get up from their machines, and the shop is suddenly quiet:

S'ershaynt mir di shap in der mitog-tsayt shtunde
A blutike shlakhtfeld, ven dort vert gerut:
Arum un arum ze ikh lign harugim,

Es liyaremt fun dr'erd dos fargosene blut . . .
Eyn vayle, un bald vert gepoykt a trevoge,
Di toyte ervakhn, es lebt uf di shlakht,
Es kemfen di trupes far fremde, far fremde,
Un shtraytn un faln, un zinkn in nakht.

[At lunchtime, the shop appears to me as
a bloody battlefield at rest:
Around and around I see murdered ones,
Spilled blood wails from the ground . . .
After a short pause a call to arms is sounded,
The dead come to life, the battle is rejuvenated,
The troops struggle for strangers, for strangers,
and fight and fall and sink into night.]

Although the metaphor and language of war permeate earlier Sweatshop poems, here the battle is not so much an external fight between workers and bosses or between workers and the capitalist system, as it is an internal fight to protect the self from the dehumanizing effects of mechanized labor. Rosenfeld further shifts the ground with his invocation of the revived dead in the final lines of the stanza. In the early poems, the dead return to bring special knowledge and speak certain truths to the protagonists, whereas here the dead revive merely to die again. There is no optimistic prophecy of eventual victory. In Rosenfeld's earlier works—as well as in those of his contemporaries—the protagonists often refer to their fellow workers as "brothers," employing the language of sentimentalism to create an intimacy among the working class. The speaker of "The Sweatshop," however, views the human sacrifices of the battle as "strangers," which calls into question the validity of their efforts. Death and revival seem but another form of dehumanized mechanization.

In the following stanza, the speaker comes to understand the full, metaphorical meaning of the clock's ticking and experiences a sudden revelation:

> Ikh kuk af dem kamf-plats mit bitern tsorn,
> mit shrek, mit nekome, mit helisher payn;
> der zeyger, yetst her ikh im rikhtik, er vekt es:
> "A sof tsu di knekhtshaft, a sof zol dos zayn!"
> Er mintert in mir mayn farshtand, di gefiln,
> un vayzt vi es loyfn di shtundn ahin:
> An elender blayb ikh, vi lang ikh vel shvaygn,
> farlorn, vi lang ikh farblayb vos ikh bin. (10)

> [I look at the arena of battle with bitter rage,
> with fear, with revenge, with infernal pain;
> the clock, I now hear it correctly, it awakens:
> "An end to the slavery, there should be an end!"
> It stimulates in me my understanding, the feelings,
> and shows how the hours are running away:
> I will remain forlorn as long as I am silent,
> lost, as long as I remain what I am.]

As the speaker becomes aware of the scene before him, for the moment, he expresses his emotions in the terms of earlier Sweatshop poetry. The clock "awakens" him to his purpose: he must seek "revenge"; with "heroic pain," the speaker demands an end to the current system of "slavery." His tone grows optimistic when he realizes he has the power to change the situation, at least for himself. This self-actualization, which builds throughout the poem, reaches its climax in the first half of the concluding stanza:

> Der mentsh, velkher shloft in mir heybt on ervakhn,
> der knekht, velkher vakht in mir shloft dakht zikh ayn;
> atsind iz di rikhtike shtunde gekumen!
> A sof tsu der elent, a sof zol es zayn. (11)

[The person, who sleeps in me, begins to awaken,
the slave, who is awake in me, seems to fall asleep;
now the right time has come!
An end to sadness, there should be an end.]

The unthinking automaton-slave is roused from his stupor. Conquering his depressed immobility, the thinking, living speaker rises up in the name of the worker. His apparent victory is short-lived, however. Unlike Rosenfeld's earlier poems, "The Sweatshop" does not end on an upbeat note:

Nor plutsling—der vistle, der bos—a trevoge!
Ikh ver on dem seykhl, farges, vu ikh bin,
es tumlt, men kemft, o, mayn ikh iz farlorn,
ikh veys nit, mikh art nit, ikh bin a mashin. (11)

[But suddenly—the whistle, the boss—a call to arms!
I lose my mind, forget who I am,
there's a tumult, there's fighting, o, my "I" is lost,
I know not, I care not, I am a machine.]

Emitting a second whistle to signal the end of the brief lunch break, and the imminent return of the boss, the clock turns on the worker and exercises a deadening effect. It commands the resumption of manual labor, a command the speaker realizes he cannot disobey. Instead of a rousing call to arms that, in earlier Sweatshop poems, would summon the workers to social revolution and the destruction of the capitalist system, the clock and history appear to have switched sides and now represent the unjust system itself. Whatever hope the speaker's memory had sparked is extinguished, and he resumes work as an unthinking, unfeeling machine.

"The Sweatshop" represents a turning point in the development of Rosenfeld's poetics. With it, the poet shifts the focus of the exhortative poem from an elaboration of a specific idea to a portrait of the inner workings of the poetic speaker's mind, and its tone from optimism to the pessimism that permeates his mature Sweatshop poetry. The poet's portrayal of this inner perspective is an innovation in Yiddish poetry. By having him voice his inner thoughts, Rosenfeld sheds light on the despair of his worker-protagonist, who is resigned to the only life he will ever know, the sweatshop.

In a second, shorter poem entitled "The Sweatshop," Rosenfeld portrays this microcosm from a different perspective. Whereas the first poem takes place entirely inside the shop, the second approaches the sweatshop from the outside, locating it in the surrounding world:

Korner vey un elnt shteyt an alte hayzl:
untn iz a shenkl, oybn iz a klayzl.
Untn kumen lumpn ufton nor nevoles,
oybn kumen yidn, klogn afn goles.

Ober hekher, hekher: afn dritn gorn,
iz faran a tsimer—vey tsu zayne yorn!
Zeltn ven gevashn, zeltn ven gereynikt,
tukhlekhkeyt un blote zaynen dort fareynikt. (51)

[At the corner of Pain and Misery there stands a small old house:
On the ground floor there is a small tavern, above it a small house of study.
On the ground floor lowlifes come, interested only in disgusting things,
Above it, Jews come, wailing over the Jewish exile.

But higher, higher: on the third floor,
there is a room—it is just awful!

Seldom is it washed, seldom is it cleaned,
staleness and mud are united there.]

Here the speaker is not the poem's protagonist, but a narrator with wider awareness, if not omniscience. Rosenfeld has this narrator begin with a large picture—the place that is the center of the poem's action—and then narrow his scope to the true focal point, the sweatshop on the third floor.

The poet then describes his setting, a metaphor for the existence of the immigrant laborer. By locating the sweatshop in a *hayzl* (small house), a common Yiddish euphemism for brothel, he evokes both the insignificance of the workers' existence and the moral depravity that pervades their workplace. This third-floor sweatshop contains the worst elements of its downstairs neighbors—the staleness of the house of study, the mud of the tavern; it is seldom "gereynikt" (washed), a word that means both "cleaned" and "purified."

Here as in the first poem, Rosenfeld adheres to strict prosodic conventions, and presses them to serve the meaning of his poem. His rigid rhythmic structure and overpowering meter underline the capitalist system's control over the workers. Each of the poem's four stanzas has four lines, cast in iambic hexameter; each line is divided into equal sections of three feet—corresponding to the meanings of the sections. Moreover, many of the individual words are themselves iambs, such as in the first line of the second stanza, which locates the sweatshop: "Ober hekher, hekher: afn dritn gorn" (But higher, higher: on the third floor).

The strict meter of this poem carries an additional meaning. Rosenfeld uses poetic rigidity to mirror his fatalistic view of shop life. The future for these immigrant shop workers is, like the consistent prosody, predictable. In the final stanza, the speaker declares:

Dortn geyt arum zikh Motke parkh a beyzer,
shpilndik di role fun a gantsn keyzer,

den er iz der mayster un di shap iz zayne,
un men muz im folgn, folgn on a tayne. (51)

[There Motke the Boor walks around, always angry,
playing the role of an emperor,
then he is the master and the shop is his,
and one must obey him, obey without complaint.]

Just as there are set rules from which the poem may not devi-
ate, so, too, according to the speaker, there are guidelines that gov-
ern the world of the immigrant shop worker. Whereas Rosenfeld
in his earlier poetry—and his contemporaries in their exhortative
poems—relies on rhetoric to express his message, in his mature
works, he exploits poetic form to organize and emphasize his
meanings. Moreover, by presenting the shop as an autocracy in
which the boss is king and the workers subjects, the poet further
compounds his message of despair.

The idea that the sweatshop is the only available avenue of
employment forsocial and economic system. With the exception of
several poems on the coal-mining industry—which Rosenfeld
represents as the sweatshop transposed to a rural setting—the ma-
jority of his protagonists work in the sweatshops of New York.
Rosenfeld appropriates this historical reality, in "The Sweatshop"
poems and elsewhere, highlighting the oppressive nature of
sweatshop labor, which produced "opgetserte mener, opgetserte
vayber" (emaciated husbands, emaciated wives).

In his mature Sweatshop poems, Rosenfeld often comple-
ments and intensifies melodrama with sentimentalism; in doing
so, he commonly makes use of the family. As Peter Brooks explains
in *The Melodramatic Imagination*,[21] family members such as father,
mother, child assume primary psychic roles in melodrama and express basic psychic conditions. The importance of family, notes
Joanne Dobson in "Reclaiming Sentimental Literature," is tied to

the very existence of the family members. Because the self is always portrayed and envisioned in terms of its relationship to other people—particularly immediate family members—the greatest disaster in sentimental literature is death, not because the character who dies is no more, but rather because death represents a total and final end to the connections between people. These bonds constitute the core of life's meaning in the sentimental mode and therefore, "the greatest threat is the tragedy of separation, of severed human ties: the death of a child, lost love, failed or disrupted family connections. . ."[22] Such disruption is a central motif in Rosenfeld's mature Sweatshop poems.

The clearest manifestation of this motif is Rosenfeld's "Mayn yingele" (My Boy), a widely anthologized poem so popular it was set to music and became a well-known folk song among Yiddish speakers. In this highly sentimental poem, the speaker laments how little time he has had to spend with his son:

Di arbet traybt mikh fri aroys
un lozt mikh shpet tsurik;
O, fremd iz mir mayn eygn layb!
O, fremd mayn kinds a blik! (16)

[Work chases me away early
and dismisses me late;
Oh, strange to me is my own flesh and blood!
Oh, strange my child's gaze!]

Rosenfeld emphasizes the distance between father and son by repeating the word *fremd* (strange), implying that the two are strangers to each other. Because the poem's father is never at home when the child is awake, he fears that his son does not know him. Returning late from work as usual, the father steals over to the child's bed:

Ikh shtey ba zayn gelegerl
un ze, un her, un sha!
A troym bavegt di lipelekh:
"O, vu iz, vu iz pa?"

Ikh kush di bloye eygelekh,
zey efnen zikh—"o, kind!"
Zey ze'en mikh, zey ze'en mikh,
un shlisn zikh geshvind. (17)

[I stand by his bed
and see, and hear, and shh!
A dream moves his lips:
"Oh, where is, where is Pa?"

I kiss his little blue eyes,
they open—"Oh, child!"
They see me, they see me,
and then close quickly.]

Here Rosenfeld creates further distance between father and son by making the child's eyes, not the child himself, the active agent. The boy does not open his eyes; rather, "they open." He does not see his father; rather, "they" do. This idea is reinforced in the next stanza when the father addresses his child, and the boy repeats the line from his dream, "Oh, where is, where is Pa?" demonstrating that he is in fact fast asleep and does not acknowledge his father's presence.

Ikh blayb tseveytikt un tseklemt,
farbitert un ikh kler:
"Ven du ervakhst a mol, mayn kind,
gefinstu mikh nit mer." (18)

[I remain pained and depressed,
embittered and I think:
"When you wake up one day, my child,
you'll find me here no more."]

The closing stanza accentuates the gulf between the two: the
father laments that he will likely die before reconciling with his
son.

Sentimentalism plays a central role in the development of
Rosenfeld's poetics of despair, particularly in ballads such as "My
Boy," where personal emotion is a key element of the poem's
meaning. Early in his career, Rosenfeld sentimentalized the ballad
form, which would later become a vehicle for existential investiga-
tion in his hands. For example, in "Di muter an dos kind" (The
Mother to Her Child),[23] a mother warns her son of the "evil system" in which the rich oppress the poor. Her repetitive lament,
framed in eight-line stanzas—doubled ballad quatrains—reaches
its climax in the poem's ninth and final stanza:

Her, mayn kind, mit a reynem zinen
als vos ikh zog,
du vest darayn fil gutn gefinen,
erbe kind vos ikh farmog:
fun sotsialismus di ide
dos zol dayn erbteyl zayn,
nur lerne gut un fershtey,
dan vestu zen dos likhtike shayn![24]

[Listen, my child, with a pure mind,
to all that I say,
you will find much good within it,
inherit, my child, what I possess:
the idea of socialism
this should be your legacy,

but learn it well and understand it,
then you will see the bright light!]

Whereas Rosenfeld politicizes the ballad in "The Mother to Her Child," investing a mother's lullaby with a radical agenda, in his mature poetry, he depoliticizes and sentimentalizes it. His later balladic speakers do not preach socialism; rather, they bemoan the difficult existence of the immigrant shop worker. Unlike the narrator in the popular or traditional ballad, who is a detached relater of events,[25] the narrator of the sentimental ballad is concerned with and passes judgment on the situation. This genre enjoys a strong tradition in both American and Yiddish letters, best exemplified by the nineteenth-century railroad ballads and by the poetry of Morris Vinchevsky.[26]

In "My Boy," however, Rosenfeld not only sentimentalizes the ballad; he also expands its scope. Unlike other sentimental ballads in Yiddish literature, the protagonist of "My Boy" speaks in the first person. He goes beyond relating and commenting on the action to play a central role in the poem, which serves as both a forum for the speaker to express his sadness at the severed connection between himself and his son and an examination of the speaker himself. Furthermore, in addition to its basic themes of toil and disconnection, the poem's form played a crucial role in its tremendous popularity among Rosenfeld's audience. Based on the model of the Yiddish folk song, every stanza of "My Boy" contains four lines, with an ABCB rhyme scheme, and every two lines of the poem form a syntactic unity concluded by a rhyme.[27] Indeed, soon after he wrote it, Rosenfeld set this poem to music, and it quickly assumed the status of an anonymous, Yiddish folk song.

The theme of toil as a disintegrating force within the family pervades Rosenfeld's mature Sweatshop poetry, particularly his sentimental ballads. In "In shap un der heym" (At the Shop and at

Home), the speaker describes the scene he typically encounters when he returns from work each evening:

> Di shtub iz farvist un anshvign,
> ikh kuk zikh arum mit a hust:
> mayn oreme froy ze ikh lign,
> zi blondzhet fun kholem a nign,
> dos pitsele troymt ba ir brust. (23)

> [The house is laid waste and silenced,
> I look around with a cough:
> I see my poor wife laying there,
> a tune rambles from her dream,
> the little one dreams at her breast.]

Whereas the protagonist in "My Boy" has a waking relationship with his wife who informs him of their son's activities during the day, the speaker in "At the Shop and at Home" has no waking connection with any members of his family.

It is significant that in both poems the protagonists notice their family members "dreaming," not merely sleeping. The sleep of the children is deep and restful: in "My Boy," the child is barely disturbed when his father kisses his eyes; in "At the Shop and at Home," the nursing infant has fallen asleep while feeding. The shop workers, performing difficult physical labor, often for fourteen hours a day, six days a week, idealize sleep. These protagonists envy this type of rest as they live lives of unrest with little respite.

Throughout "At the Shop and at Home," the speaker makes reference to his suffering body, using terms such as *krank* (sick), *gebrokhn* (broken), and *vunden* (wounds) to describe his deteriorating condition. He is pessimistic as he expresses his concern that death may be an impending prospect:

Vos tuen zey bald take morgn,
vi shnel der fardiner zey felt?
O, ver vet zey leyen, tsi borgn?
Zogar mit dos klenste bazorgn?
Vu blaybt zey a fraynd af der velt? (23)

[What would they do tomorrow,
if their breadwinner were gone?
Oh, who would lend to them, who would they borrow from?
Even with the smallest of needs?
Where would they have a friend in the world?]

Here more than relationships and communication among family members are at stake. The protagonist's death would likely lead to the death of his family members; the disintegration of the family has reached its ultimate conclusion.

Although "At the Shop and at Home" presents an obvious example of death pervading a family household, thereby threatening the basic connections that give life its very meaning in this type of literature, there are other, more subtle instances of the disintegration of the family in Rosenfeld's mature Sweatshop poetry. In "Mit mayn kind" (With My Child), for example, as the protagonist and his son go for a leisurely stroll through their neighborhood, the child asks his father to purchase several inexpensive items they pass, such as a little toy or a piece of fruit. The father is greatly upset that he cannot afford to purchase these small presents for his child and, as a result, he decides not to take his son along when he goes on walks. The father's shame and sadness thus further limit the minimal amount of free time that he has to spend with his child, and the distance between father and child grows even greater.

Rosenfeld provides a more straightforward and literal account of the splitting of familial bonds in "Di oreme gezind" (The

Poor Family). In this poem, a homeless family is brought before a judge on the charge of vagrancy:

> O, zeyer zind iz zeyer groys,
> iz gevaldik, tsum ershtoynen!
> Zey hobn mer keyn heym far zikh,
> keyn dire, vu tsu voynen.
> Zey kukn af dem rikhter yetst,
> zey kenen di grimasn,
> zey veysn shoyn dem vildn psak
> far vandln in di gasn. (52)

> [Oh, their sin is great,
> it's frightening, astounding!
> They no longer have their own home,
> no dwelling, no place to live.
> They now look at the judge,
> they know his grimaces,
> they already know the absurd sentence
> for wandering in the streets.]

Here, as in several of Rosenfeld's other sentimental ballads, the speaker distinguishes himself from his traditional counterpart: he comments on the situation, bridging the distance between speaker and narrative, while using the rhetoric of the earlier exhortative poems. He reveals his own feelings about the situation, expressing his emotions in strong terms. Rosenfeld uses alliteration ("zeyer zind iz zeyer," "zey . . . zey . . . zey") to reinforce his speaker's sarcasm, to show that he thinks the family's "sin" is not especially "great," but rather, the exact opposite. To make this sarcasm and social critique more potent, Rosenfeld takes the idea of a home and emotionally shrinks it through an orchestrated series of synonyms, moving directly from the warm and familiar *heym* (home), to the colder, less familiar *dire* (dwelling), to the completely neutral *vu tsu voynen* (place to live). As the family's "sin" grows—it ɪs "very big," then "terrible," then "shocking"—their "home" emotionally shrinks until they have nothing. The poet relies on heavy-handed sarcasm and poetic technique to deliver his message, but it is in the poem's final stanza that he reveals its exhortative character. When the judge orders the couple's children be taken from their custody, the speaker forthrightly voices his disdain for the entire judicial process:

Der mishpet, er iz oysgeredt,
un ken er zayn nokh vilder?
O, dopelt flukh af der sistem,
vos shaft azelkhe bilder! (55)

[The sentence, it has been pronounced,
and could it be any more absurd?
Oh, a double curse on the system,
that produces such images!]

Instead of focusing on the human and emotional aspects of the family's disintegration, the exhortative speaker-agitator pronounces on the "system." The people who make up this family are portrayed, not as individuals, but as generic players, as "images" that represent the unfortunate products of society and an unjust system. Rosenfeld adapts the ballad to his purposes, integrating his earlier rhetoric and reverting to the model of the exhortative poem.

"The Poor Family" illustrates melodrama's black-and-white understanding of existence. In it, the system, represented by the judge, is evil and the victimized family is good. The judge is not merely an upper-class member of society who is forced to play his role in this unjust system, but an enemy of the working class, to whom he shows no sympathy. Conversely, the family members are completely innocent victims of the capitalist system—they can hardly be blamed for their vagrancy, the speaker is quick to note. This portrayal of innocence pervades Rosenfeld's Sweatshop poems, whose poor protagonists, particularly young women, are presented as pure, decent victims of the unfair and sinister system that destroys families, sundering the crucial bonds his protagonists depend on to live.

In "Di ershte veydzhes" (The First Wages), the narrator tells the story of a worker dying from the prospect of a final devastating loss:

> Zayn froy, ir hot di shvindzukht
> in grub shoyn lang geshlept,
> un fun di kinder ale,
> dos yingste kind nor lebt. (41)

> [His wife, tuberculosis
> dragged her to her grave long ago,
> and among all the children,
> only the youngest one is still alive.]

As he does throughout his mature Sweatshop poetry, Rosenfeld takes a common occurrence among immigrant workers and personalizes it within a melodramatic-sentimental framework. Tuberculosis was a death sentence in turn-of-the-century New York, particularly on the Lower East Side, where the highly contagious disease spread rapidly among shop workers and their families who lived and worked in close quarters.

Because the father is near death, his only surviving child—a young, innocent girl—is forced to quit school and work to support what is left of her family:

> Zi hot di shul farlozn,
> dos lebns hekhste glik—

der tate ligt a goyses
un zi iz in fabrik.

Zi muz, zi muz fardinen,
dos iz der letster plan;
zi muz di hoyz farzorgn,
dem oremn, krankn man. (42)

[She left school,
life's greatest joy—
her father lays dying
and she is in the factory.

She must, she must earn,
this is the last resort;
she must take care of the house,
[and of] the poor, sick man.]

Rosenfeld describes this situation in typically melodramatic terms. Because of her father's illness, the girl is forced to abandon her education, which the poet presents in idealized language as "life's greatest joy." The speaker elaborates on this extreme situation in fittingly extreme terms: working in the factory is the daughter's "last resort." The speaker implies that if the girl does not find employment, she and her father will join the rest of their family in the grave. Although he heightens the language and exaggerates the tone of the narrative, Rosenfeld still bases his poem on sociohistorical reality. In truth, a school-age girl in this setting would have few opportunities for employment outside of the factory.

In the subsequent stanza, the speaker highlights the girl's innocence:

Dos iz ir ershte probe,
dos iz ir ershte vokh,
ir ershter trit in knekhtshaft,

ir ershter gang in yokh. (42)

[This is her first test,
this is her first week,
her first step into slavery,
her first entry into oppression.]

The anaphora of this stanza—"her first"—is typical of sentimental literature. In his later Sweatshop poems, Rosenfeld often
repeats phrases or sentences throughout his poems to reinforce
certain ideas. In the case of "The First Wages," the speaker uses
this literary device not only to underline the girl's inexperience,
but also to stress the irony of the situation: it is her first working experience, but also her "last resort." The poet's use of irony is also
apparent in his exhortative rhetoric. By calling factory work "slavery" and "oppression," the speaker betrays his social conscience
and the exhortative character of the poem. Unlike Rosenfeld's earlier exhortative poems, however, "The First Wages" does not conclude on a positive note. As he lies on his deathbed—a common
setting in both melodramatic and sentimental poetry—the father
is ruminating on his bitter life when the door springs open and his
daughter rushes in with her first week's salary. The girl announces
that she has earned four dollars, and tells her father of all the great
plans she has for this money. She then saves what she perceives to
be the best piece of news for last:

Mayn bos iz gut un eydl,
er hot gezogt, der gvir:
Du bist a sheyne meydl,
vest nitslekh zayn far mir. (44)

[My boss is kind and noble,
that rich man said:

You are a beautiful girl,
you will be useful to me.]

Her naïve enthusiasm is quickly squelched by her father, who understands all too well what the boss's "nitslekh" (useful) really means. The motif of seduction is well represented in Rosenfeld's Sweatshop poems, and here it literally kills the dying man to see what is in store for his daughter. In the final stanza, Rosenfeld uses alliteration *(ts, s, es)* to describe the father's final, tortured moments:

Dos tsitert oys der goyses,
zayn letses vort atsind
un af di lipn shtarbt es:
"mayn kind . . . mayn eyntsik kind!" (44)

[The dying man now shudders
(to breathe) his last words
and they die on his lips:
"My child . . . my only child!"] ˙

The hissing of this stanza conveys the physical expiration of the man. The girl's naïve and optimistic hopes are dashed by her father's death, which ends the poem on a pessimistic note. Rosenfeld thus resolves the suspense created with the incremental repetition of the words "her first" in the earlier stanza. Although her first week of work may have felt like a success, it now ends in abject failure.

The young woman, almost always presented in chaste terms, is a recurring character in Rosenfeld's Sweatshop poems. Take, for example, "Di kale fun di berg" (The Bride of the Mountains), an atypical Sweatshop poem set in the coalfields of the Alleghenies. At the beginning of the poem, the speaker introduces the reader to the lone survivor of a mining disaster that has killed her father and young bridegroom:

> Dokh di viste koylnmine
> dort iz blut geflosn.
> Untn ligt der guter alter
> un zayn tokhters khosn. (48–49)

> [The desolate coal mine,
> blood flowed there.
> The good old man lies underground
> and so does his daughter's fiancé.]

In a common melodramatic and sentimental trope, the protagonist is an orphan, whose disconnection and loneliness is compounded by the death of her fiancé before her wedding day. Now living in isolation in the mountains, she finds her only consolation in sleep, where she dreams that her father—a "good" man—and fiancé come back to life. In sleep, she can resume her former life, at least for a time.

This leads to another prevalent motif in Rosenfeld's proletarian poetry, namely, the presentation of work-induced death within a dream sequence or fantasy. In earlier poems such as "The Dream on the Brooklyn Bridge" and "Night Thoughts," the poet uses a dream to redeem the life of the worker and to inspire him to change a desperate situation. In Rosenfeld's mature poems, although the dream sequence also represents an escape from the referential world, it does not convey the same hope. In "The Bride of the Mountains," the misery of the woman's lonely life is relieved only by a dream, where her father and fiancé are joined by a group of dead musicians, as well as other members of the deceased mining community, for a midnight celebration. Soon, however, the guests disappear and the bride and groom are left alone for a brief moment:

Un zey blaybn un zey tantsn
ruhik, keyner shtert nit,
biz es git a vunk fun ergets,
un der khosn vert nit.

Do shpringt uf dem toytns kale:
"O, di mentshnshekhter!"
un farshvindet in di berger
mit a vild gelekhter. (50)

[And they remain and they dance
peacefully, no one disturbs them,
until he is summoned from somewhere,
and the bridegroom disappears.

Here the dead one's bride jumps up:
"Oh, you butchers-of-men!"
and disappears into the mountains
with wild laughter.]

In Rosenfeld's earlier works, the dead rise from their graves to interact with the poems' characters. These meetings are purposive and productive, leaving the protagonists with a new awareness and appreciation of life. In "The Bride of the Mountains," however, the young woman cannot find consolation even in her dreams: these nocturnal experiences only worsen her lonely condition without offering any redemption.

Like many of Rosenfeld's mature Sweatshop poems, "The Bride of the Mountains" is a sentimentalized ballad. The speaker involves himself in the narrative through his comments, and describes the protagonist in sentimental terms:

Un zayn frume, sheyne tokhter,
akh, vos ken zayn erger?
Vandlt mit a gayst a krankn

af di shtume berger. (49)

[And his pious, beautiful daughter,
oh, what could be worse?
She wanders with a sick spirit
over the silent mountains.]

Thus the girl is no mere mountain bride, but "pious" and "beautiful"; she "wanders with a sick spirit." With "silent mountains," the speaker implies, at best, that nature would like to respond to the girl's crisis, but cannot speak, and at worst, that nature is indifferent to the girl and even complicit in her suffering: leaving the mountain bride to languish in her remote country surroundings.

The rural setting of this poem allows Rosenfeld to express a central theme of his oeuvre, namely, the distance between workers and nature. As opposed to his earlier works, where nature operates in harmony with the worker, in his mature Sweatshop poems, nature becomes an unattainable ideal; workers can never enjoy the natural world. This motif highlighted in the mock pastoral "Fartsveyflung" (Despair):

Bald hobn di beymer un blumen farblit,
bald endikt der foygl der letster zayn lid,
bald zet men nor kvorim arum un arum!
O, vi volt ikh velen a shmek ton a blum,
a shlung ton khotsh, eyder es shtarbt op dos groz,
af felder bagrinte dem vinteles bloz!
"In feld vilstu zayn, vu s'iz luftig un grin?
nisht koshe, men vet dikh shoyn brengn ahin!" (19)

[Soon the trees and flowers will have finished blooming,
soon the bird will have sung his last song,
soon all that will be seen will be graves all around!

Oh, how I would love to smell a flower,
just one sniff, before the grass dies out,
in green fields, the blow of the little wind!
"You want to be in the field where it's airy and green?
Do not worry, you will soon be brought there!"]

Rosenfeld delivers his message through two voices. The first is that of a worker who longs for a respite from the sweatshop in nature, and the second is an unnamed, sarcastic voice that ironically assures the worker he can soon enjoy nature—in death.

"Despair" parodies the pastoral poem, specifically, the traditional form first used by Theocritus in his *Idylls,* in which couplets or verses are spoken in turn by two different speakers, with the second speaker reinforcing and often improving upon the ideas of the first. In Rosenfeld's poem, however, the second voice undercuts that of the first, specifically through a use of double meaning. In the above stanza, the second voice plays on the word *feld,* which in Yiddish literally means "field" but is also a common euphemism for "cemetery."

This poem is also a clear example of Rosenfeld's artful use of regulated prosody. Each stanza in "Despair" is eight lines long, with an AABBCCDD rhyme scheme. As in the first and more celebrated "The Sweatshop" poem, Rosenfeld turns to the amphibrach in "Despair," but manipulates it in a manner that reflects the thematic concern of this poem. Each line contains four amphibrachs—three full and one curtailed—for a total of eleven syllables. Rosenfeld reinforces this curtailment of the meter by ending each line with a masculine rhyme, thereby creating a conflict between the soft, musical, flowing of the line and its abrupt ending. The theme the poet drives home here—indeed, the one central to most of his mature Sweatshop poems—is that of death and the brevity of the worker's monotonous life.

Rosenfeld uses other poetic devices besides meter to convey

monotony. In the first line of the stanza above, he employs a *b* sound—"bald," "hobn," "beymer," "blumen," "farblit"—to reinforce the already pronounced deadening effect of his poem. In the same stanza, he also alliterates, using and repeating words that begin with an *f* sound (the Yiddish letter *fey*):

> O, darf men nit ruen khotsh eyn tog in vokh,
> a tog mer nit fray zayn fun shreklekhen yokh?
> fargesn dem bos, dem farbisenem mruk,
> zayn finstere mine, zayn shreklekhn kuk,
> fargesn di shap un dem formans geshrey,
> fargesn di knekhtshaft, fargesn dem vey,
> "fargesn zikh vilstu un ruen dertsu?
> Nit zorg zikh, ot bald vestu geyn in dayn ru!" (19)

> [Must one not rest even one day of the week,
> to be free at least one day from the dreadful yoke?
> To forget the boss, the embittered killjoy,
> his dark face, his frightening look,
> to forget the shop and the foreman's shouting,
> to forget slavery, to forget woe?
> "You wish to forget yourself and be rested as well?
> Do not worry, you will soon go to your rest!"]

This stanza is extremely repetitive, as is the entire poem. The word the poet repeats most, for greatest emphasis, is *fargesn* (to forget). The innocent first voice (worker) longs to forget the oppressive environment of the shop and to enjoy a bit of rest. Seizing upon this key word, the malicious second voice assures the worker he will soon be allowed to forget all in his eternal rest.

The sarcastic tone of this poem highlights the great pessimism that pervades Rosenfeld's mature Sweatshop poetry and differentiates it from his previous works. Instead of rebelling, as do Rosenfeld's earlier, heroic protagonists, his later protagonists simply lament their status as victims. This pessimism is more intense than that of the typical melodramatic poem, which "plays out the force of that anxiety . . . with the eventual victory of virtue."[28] Peter Brooks outlines the five stages of melodrama: (1) the presentation of virtue-as-innocence, almost always represented by a woman; (2) the introduction of a menace or obstacle that places virtue in peril; (3) the reign of evil for the large part; (4) the resistance of virtue fallen; and (5) the public recognition and elimination of evil and the reward of virtue.[29] Rosenfeld treats the issue of virtue fallen in works such as "The First Wages," "The Bride of the Mountains," "Di farfirte" (Led Astray), and "Vuhin?" (Whither?). These poems stop short of eradicating evil, however, and do not redeem fallen virtue. This idea finds extended expression in "Whither?" addressed "Tsu a meydele" (To a Girl):

> Vuhin, vuhin, du sheynes kind?
> Di velt iz nokh nisht ofn!
> O, ze, vi shtil do iz arum!
> Fartog, di gasn shteyen shtum,
> vuhin, vuhin, azoy geshvind?
> Yetst iz dokh gut tsu shlofn:
> di blumen troymn dokh nokh, zest?
> Es shvaygt nokh yeder feyglnest,
> vuhin fort traybt es dikh atsind?
> Vu loyfstu, zog, baginen?
> "Ikh gey fardinen!" (30)

> [Whither, whither, you beautiful child?
> The world is not yet open!
> Oh, see how quiet it is all around!
> It's not yet day, the streets are mute,
> whither, whither, are you going so quickly?
> Now is a good time for sleep;
> even the flowers are still dreaming, see?

Each bird's nest is still silent,
whither are you being driven now?
Where are you running, tell me, at dawn?
"I am going to earn a living!"]

The first stanza of this two-stanza poem, like the second, is precisely ordered, with the first nine lines following a melodious and full rhyming pattern of ABCCABDDA. Furthermore, seven of these lines (all except lines two and six) are composed in iambic tetrameter (four pairs of unstressed and stressed syllables). In addition, lines two and six, each composed in iambic trimeter, are further distinguished by their exclusive "B" rhyme and feminine ending.

Vuhin, vuhin, du sheynes kind,
zo shpet ba nakht shpatsirn?
Aleyn durkh finsternish un kelt!
Un ales rut, es shvaygt di velt,
vuhin fort trogt es dikh der vint?
Du vest nokh dokh fariren!
Koym hot der tog dir nit gelakht,
vos ken dir helfn den di nakht?
Zi iz dokh shtum un toyb un blind!
Vuhin mit laykhtn zinen?
"Ikh gey fardinen!" (30–31)

[Whither, whither, you beautiful child,
are you strolling so late at night?
Alone through darkness and cold!
And everything is at rest, the world is silent,
where is the wind carrying you?
You will yet go astray!
The day could hardly keep from mocking you,
how then can the night help?

It is, after all, deaf and dumb and blind!
Whither are you going so recklessly?
"I am going to earn a living!"]

In both stanzas, the speaker witnesses the girl rushing off when, in his opinion, it is not normal to rush, first, early in the morning and, then, late at night, both times of quiet and darkness. In both, Rosenfeld uses the shortened last two lines—the "E" lines of the stanza's ABCCABDDAEE rhyme scheme—and the girl's brief, businesslike answer to mimic and emphasize her rushing. In the first stanza, although the time of the day is particularly early—before sunrise—it is not an unusual hour for an immigrant shop worker to commute to his or her job. The girl's answer to the speaker's main question, "Whither?"—"I am going to earn a living"—would thus arouse no particular suspicion among speaker and readers.

When in the second stanza, however, the speaker sees the girl in the street "so late at night" and again asks her where she is going, her identical answer to his question of that morning alerts readers to the virtual certainty that the girl's second job is degrading. Before her second answer, Rosenfeld uses meter and rhyme to make clear exactly what she does.

In lines two and six of the stanzas, the "B" rhymes and the only two lines in the first nine of each stanza that end in feminine rhymes, Rosenfeld vaguely hints at (first stanza) then reveals (second stanza) the girl's second, shameful profession. In the first stanza, where it is not yet clear that the subject is a prostitute, the poet's prosodic hints are correspondingly opaque, both in a formal and a semantic sense. The final rhymes and the semantic connection of lines two and six with the final line of the stanza, " 'I am going to earn a living!' " are tenuous: "ofn"-"shlofn"- " 'fardinen' " (open-sleep-earn a living). In the poem's second stanza, however, both the final rhymes and the semantic connection of the corresponding lines are much clearer: "shpatsirn"-"fariren"-" 'fardinen' " (walk-go astray-earn a living).

Rosenfeld's use of this irregular, eleven-line stanza endows the poem with an added artificiality, as well as a contrast between the poem's two characters. In the first ten lines of each stanza, Rosenfeld manipulates rhyme and meter, so that the poetic speaker's questions flow into one long-winded musing. In contrast, he allows the girl only one short line, " 'Ikh gey fardinen!' " (I am going to earn a living!), which she repeats. Rosenfeld thus accentuates—not only through language, but also through prosody—the difference between the bourgeois moralist who has the time to stand on the street and sermonize, and the hardworking girl who has only the time to deliver a curt, businesslike reply as she rushes off to support herself.

The young girl represents virtue-as-innocence-fallen and is a clear casualty of the capitalist system. The fact that she is not an old or experienced prostitute, but rather a young woman, adds to the pathos of the poem as we see someone who has probably only recently turned to this second occupation out of desperation. An older prostitute would not fit the melodramatic structure of "innocence-as-virtue" as well as the young girl does.

Another example of virtue-as-innocence-fallen is the poem "Led Astray," in which a shop girl addresses her boss's son, a boy who has seduced and then quickly rejected her:

> Gedenkstu, vi du host mir libe geshvorn?
> Gegrint hot der eplboym tsvishn di korn.
> Der feygl hot ruik geblikt fun di tsvaygn
> un ales arum iz gelegn in shvaygn . . .
> O, ver hot es damols gevust dayn kavone?
> Geshtumt hobn himl un erd un levone,
> ven du host geshvorn far mir mit a fayer,
> az eybik farblaybstu mayn eyntsig getrayer. (45)

[Do you remember how you swore your love to me?
The apple tree blossomed among the rye.
The bird peacefully looked on from the branches
and everything around lay in silence . . .
Oh, who then knew your true intentions?
Earth, sky, and moon were silent,
when you swore to me with fire,
that you would be my only one forever.]

The girl laments her deception on the moonlit evening when the young man swore false devotion to her, which Rosenfeld makes seem all the more false against a Romantic nature background he paints with ironic exaggeration.

As she describes her violation, her words ring sharply true, however elevated their tone:

O, dan in dayn umreyner vuntsh dir gelungen,
du host in mayn heyliktum frekh ayngedrungen,
mayn ere geroybt un mayn lebn tsurisn,
mikh biter baleydikt un enlekh farshmisn. (45)

[Oh, then as your impure wish was crowned with success,
you brazenly penetrated my holiness,
robbed my honor and tore apart my life,
horribly insulted as well as whipped me.]

Rosenfeld, in a manifestation of a motif common in his Sweatshop poems, suggests that the girl was betrayed not only by the boy, but also by nature. We saw above in "Whither?" that the day is "silent" and the night "deaf and dumb and blind" to the young prostitute's desperate situation. Here, in "Led Astray," when the boy spoke false, sweet words to the girl to seduce her, "earth, sky, and moon were silent." This silence of the natural world as she is led astray and violated reinforces the alienation of the protagonist.

Furthermore, the underlying message of this poem—as well as that of most of Rosenfeld's mature Sweatshop poems—is that this unfair violence is the way of the world. Poor shop girls are at the mercy of rich boys: this is the natural order of things within the sweatshop system—the only life Rosenfeld's protagonists know—and cannot be challenged.

In "The Old and the New Morris Rosenfeld," Moyshe-Leyb Halpern criticizes "Led Astray" as an example of cheap and sensationalized sentiment. He argues that the older poet should have chosen a more common, realistic event as the plot for this poem; after all, he posits, there is so much that could be taken from a shop girl's life; there is no need to invent such an uncommon plot. According to Halpern, a poet has only to open his eyes and myriads of images will fly by; the true artist need merely let his light shine on these images to present them as poetry.[30]

Although everyday events in the life of a young woman in a sweatshop, such as her longing for her mother in the old country, or her secret love for a fellow shop worker, may present a more common scenario than the intraclass seduction in "Led Astray," it is the very uncommonness of this scenario that is essential to Rosenfeld's poetics. As Peter Brooks writes, in the melodramatic mode, "things and gestures of the real world cease to be themselves and become vehicles of metaphors whose tenor suggests another kind of reality."[31] Significant characters and events are necessarily metaphoric because they refer to the Manichaean battle played out beneath the surface of reality, in the deeper, essential realm that Brooks calls the "moral occult."

Thus hyperbole and exceptional situations are necessary tools in melodrama. If the main function of melodrama is "to invest in its renderings of life a sense of memorability and significance,"[32] then Halpern's criticism of Rosenfeld's poetics would seem to miss the point. For Rosenfeld, the seduction of virtue-as-innocence is a metaphor for the destruction of life; it represents another variation on the theme of the murderous nature of the sweatshop system, which kills its victims both literally and symbolically.

Rosenfeld, as we have seen, employs the death metaphors to emphasize the destructiveness of the sweatshop system in his oeuvre, He again engages this motif in "Afn toytn-gortn" (In the Garden of the Dead), where a *bal kholem* (dream master), a type of host and guide, carries the speaker through a cemetery at night. In his dream, the speaker sees the graves of rich and poor alike and thinks, at first, that, in death, there is finally equality between bosses and workers: "Do lign di gute, do lign di shlekhte, / do ruhen di knekht vi di srores" (68). [There lie the good, there lie the bad, / there rest the slaves as well as the masters.]

Then he notices that the graves of the rich are decorated with flowers, whereas the poor have none. Suddenly, a poor man bursts from his grave and thunders that the flowers on the rich man's grave belong to him, the poor man, as the fruits of his labor:

"O, nit nor di blumen aleyn zaynen mayne,
di breter zogar fun zayn oren.

"Un nit nor di breter aleyn fun zayn oren.
Takhrikhim, oykh ir zayt nit zayne!
Dos hot er durkh mir, durkh mayn oreme pratse,
yo, ales un ales iz mayne!"

Nokhdem iz der toyter aruf in der luftn
mit koyles. "Dos vet aykh nokh kostn!"
Un hot zayne finger in foystn farbrokhn,
un hot af der velt zikh farmostn. (71)

["Oh, not only are the flowers themselves mine,
but even the boards of his coffin.

"And not only the boards of his coffin.
Shrouds, you do not belong to him either!
He has these things through me, through my poor toil,
yes, all and all is mine!"

Then, the dead man flew up into the sky
with cries. "This will cost you yet!"
And he clenched his fingers into fists,
and threatened the world.]

The poor man's cries are for naught; his final threat rings pathetic. Clearly, the worker will not find the moral justice he seeks; he remains powerless to effect change, even in the afterlife. Whereas, in his earlier poems, the dead bring hope of a better world to inspire the living, in this and other mature Sweatshop poems, Rosenfeld uses the realm of the dead merely as a metaphor for the living. Death is but another rhetorical device to argue that the rich live by robbing the poor, and there is no way to change this natural order.

"In the Garden of the Dead" was first published in *Di blumenkete* under the title "Tsvishn di toyte" (Among the Dead). As it appears here and in various collected works, the poem differs only in its last stanza, which reads:

Far shrekenish hob ikh ervakht fun mayn kholem,
dokh klingt mir in oyer di tayne:
"O, nit nor di blumen aleyn zaynen gneyve,
nor ales un ales iz mayne." (71)

[Frightened, I awoke from my dream,
but the complaint still rings in my ear:
"Oh, not only are the flowers stolen goods,
but all and all is mine."]

In "Among the Dead," this stanza reads:

Un ales iz farshvundn fun mayne oygn;
dokh hob ikh nit fargesn di tayne:
"Nit di blumen aleyn iz geganvet,
zondern ales ales, iz zayne." [33]

[And then everything disappeared before my eyes;
but still I did not forget the complaint:
"Not only are the flowers stolen,
but all, all is his."]

Both works end with the speaker's remembered quotation of
the dead man, but the earlier poem's quotation is a paraphrase.
Despite the presence of quotation marks, the speaker speaks own
words, not the dead worker's, whereas in the poem's later, canonized version, the speaker directly quotes the dead man. This seemingly minor transformation has a major effect on the poem,
darkening it with pessimism. By not overtly supporting the dead
worker's complaint, the speaker emphasizes his own despair and,
by extension, that of the entire working class.

Although, to serve his ends, Rosenfeld subverts the exhortative poem here and throughout his mature Sweatshop poems, on
occasion, he turns to it in a more traditional manner. The clearest
instance of this is "Di royte behole" (The Red Panic), the poet's
moving tribute to the victims of the devastating Triangle Shirtwaist Factory fire of 1911, many of them young Jewish women. In
this highly emotional work, the anonymous speaker addresses
three audiences. Giving the well-known cliché an ironic twist, he
first berates America, "you golden country," for its obsession with
making money—and, by implication, for its complicity in the
deaths of these workers. He next commands his fellow Jewish
workers to commemorate the dead:

Tsindt yortsayt-likht on in di yidishe gasn!
Der brokh iz der brokh fun di yidishe masn.

Fun undzere masn farkhoyshekht un orem.
S'iz undzer levaye, yo, undzere kvorim.
S'hot undzere kinder, vey, undzere blumen,
der fayer fun undzere orems genumen.[34]

[Light memorial candles in the Jewish streets!
This misfortune is the misfortune of the Jewish masses.
Of our darkened and poor masses.
It's our funeral, yes, our graves.
It's our children, woe, our flowers,
that the fire took from our arms.]

Although the principal interlocutors of this poem—the "Jewish masses"—are the same as those of Rosenfeld's early exhortative poems, here the speaker urges his audience, not to rise up in communist revolution, but merely to light up their "darkened" lives with memorial candles. And the fire of these candles is one, not of rebellion, but of acceptance.

Still, with "The Red Panic," Rosenfeld returns to the exhortative model to intensify the rage and emotions of the speaker in the face of a great national and human catastrophe. In the final stanza, he has the speaker address his third audience, another common interlocutor of Yiddish exhortative poetry, the upper classes, through their personification "rich person":

Af dayn gevisn, raykher, undzer troyer,
af dayn gevisn undzer klog.
Es zol durkh nakht un tog
dikh shrekn der farbrenter moyer,
un undzere tekhter in di flamen
zoln dayn lebn farsamen!
Dikh zoln ba dayne freydn,
ba dayne glikn,
vergn, shtikn

undzere laydn!
Ba di simkhes fun dayne kinder
zolstu filn di klole
fun der royter behole,
un tapn vi a blinder
di vent mit shrekn,
biz di tsayt
vet brengen di tsayt
vos vet dikh farmekn![35]

[On your conscience, rich person, our sorrow,
on your conscience our lamentation.
Through night and day,
may our burnt wall haunt you,
and our daughters in the flames,
may they poison your life!
In your happy times,
in your fortunate times,
may you choke, suffocate
on our suffering!
At your children's celebrations
may you feel the curse
of The Red Panic,
and, like a blind man, feel your way
on the walls, with fear,
until time
brings the time
that will obliterate you!]

In Rosenfeld's first "The Sweatshop" poem, the bulk of the speaker's despair resides in his realization that historical forces are not on the side of the worker; the clock's whistle is not a "call to arms," but only a signal of the boss's return and the command to resume work. Historical forces have been harnessed by the capitalist system, which annihilates the worker, both in a physical and metaphorical sense.

In contrast, the speaker of "The Red Panic" warns the upper classes that it is only a matter of "time" before they are "obliterated." At first glance, this prediction seems to hark back to Rosenfeld's more optimistic earlier Sweatshop poems, in which the victory of the workers over the bosses was part of the natural progression of history. But what the speaker promises here is not a political or economic victory, but a moral one. Instead of willing the rich to lose their social and economic status—something, in his pessimism, he knows will not happen—the speaker instead curses their collective conscience and wishes them to be forever haunted by the crimes he believes they perpetrated. History is still a helping agent in this new scheme, but it does not favor either the bosses or the workers. The poet states that time will obliterate the rich, but only in the sense that it will eventually obliterate everything.

"The Red Panic" is an example of a grand, virtuosic exhortative poem in which Rosenfeld employs all manner of rhyme and meter patterns, rhetorical figures, and interlocutors to make the horror more horrific. In his mature Sweatshop poems, Rosenfeld broadens the scope of the exhortative model beyond the shifting, yet consistent prosody of poems such as "The Red Panic." For example, "Dertrunkn—a tragediye" (Drowned—A Tragedy) is a meandering monologue spoken by a "sick, pale, poor" factory worker who stands by a body of water, in "ugly, wet, and cold autumn weather." The monologue represents the worker's final speech, after which he plans to throw himself into the raging stream. "Drowned" follows in the tradition of a Hebrew poetic model widely used in the second half of the nineteenth century.[36] The model features a loquacious speaker, who often goes insane in the course of the poem, as in "Zidkiyahu ve-vet ha-pekudot" (Zedekiah in Prison) by Yehuda Leyb Gordon, one of the best-known examples, completed following a dark period in Gordon's life when his worldview, like Rosenfeld's, became pessimistic.[37] Often, too, the speaker addresses someone who is not there—such as a dead person—signaling the speaker's own agitation and growing insanity, as in "Barukh me-magenza" (Barukh of Mayence) by Shaul Tschernikhovsky.[38] Among Rosenfeld's Sweatshop poems, "Drowned" represents a rare, tour de force example in which the poet sets aside traditional prosodic conventions and applies the poetic skills he developed in the practice of his craft to their fullest. In the first stanza, he uses onomatopoeia to help set the scene for his self-titled "tragedy." When the protagonist, Mauritz, describes the weather—"Der regen patsht, es krekhtst der vint! / Ikh bin durkhgenetst" (63) [The rain slaps, the wind moans! / I am thoroughly soaked]—the onomatopoeic *patsht* (slaps) and *krekhtst* (moans) evoke the violence and deadly potential of nature, foreshadowing the poem's outcome. The mood grows more ominous so when Mauritz tells his family he must leave them:

Es rayst mikh vild avek fun aykh,
mayn bos iz shlekht, mayn lendlord raykh,
der duner rolt, es roysht di taykh. (64)

[It tears me wildly away from you,
my boss is mean, my landlord rich,
the thunder rolls, the river rushes.]

As Mauritz perceives his situation to be worsening, the storm worsens and the river—which will be the co-agent of his suicide—grows ever wilder.

Through the use of cacophony and dissonance, Rosenfeld intensifies the ugliness and menace of nature until, by the end of the poem, chaos reigns. In the final stanza, Mauritz delivers his last words before destroying himself:

A froy . . . a kind . . .
vi shreklekh! vi msukn!
Ven got iz blind,
vos zol der mentsh nokh kukn?
Shling, shtrom, mikh ayn,
a flukh dem zayn! (66–67)

[A wife . . . a child . . .
how horrible! how dangerous!
When god is blind,
what should man look after?
Swallow me, stream,
a curse on existence!]

Departing here from the prosodic regularity so characteristic of most of his Sweatshop poems, Rosenfeld heightens the chaotic and violent scene within and without his speaker-protagonist by skillfully shifting rhyme, meter, and rhythm.

The exhortative poem in Yiddish literature, particularly as it was developed by the first generation of American Yiddish poets, is, in most cases, little more than rhymed propaganda. The calls to arms of writers such as Yoysef Bovshover and Dovid Edelshtat were, almost exclusively, published in the radical Yiddish press and intended to stir readers into revolutionary action. Because these poems contained no stories, plots, or concrete situations, the only way the poets could impart a literary quality to these abstract and political works was to concentrate on form, which had to take full responsibility for making them "poetry." To this end, Yiddish poets made consistent use of conventional poetic models and stanza forms as well as regulated prosody.

Although Rosenfeld returns to the exhortative poem throughout his career, he employs it less often in his mature works than in his earlier, more optimistic works, aimed at stirring up his readers and giving them hope. The shift in the general mood of Rosen-feld's Sweatshop poetry in the 1890s is mirrored by a correspon-ding shift in genre. As his speakers become despondent, as they lose some of their collective self-confidence, Rosenfeld's poetry moves away from the exhortative to the melodramatic and senti-mental. The protagonists of his mature Sweatshop poetry are mul-tidimensional, and the poet fleshes out their personalities by endowing them with extreme emotions such as rage or grief. By focusing on the personal issues of the immigrant laborer, Rosen-feld offers his readers human portraits and not merely rhetoric.

Through artful use of melodrama and sentimental poetics, Rosenfeld's mature Sweatshop poems portray and dramatize the reality of people's lives. Although the characters are not fully indi-vidualized—indeed, at their core, they remain ideal types—they are still people, filled with emotion, in real-life situations. Once Rosenfeld became interested in them, he felt the need to transform his chosen genres, the exhortative poem and the ballad, into vehi-cles suitable for expressing the way immigrants lived and suffered in the sweatshop.

4

The "Simple" Language of the Sweatshop

When Morris Rosenfeld began his literary career in 1886, modern Yiddish literature was in its infancy and the poet's predecessors were few in number. Well-known European poets such as Shimen Frug and Y. L. Perets would soon compose original poetry in the Eastern European vernacular, but these writers were—like Vinchevsky, Bovshover, and Edelshtat—Rosenfeld's contemporaries. The only modern poetic models available to the American Yiddish poet were those of the *haskala* (Jewish Enlightenment). Rosenfeld in his earliest works fully appropriates the *haskala* model of the exhortative poem, even to the point of attacking the same targets—the religious leaders of the traditional Jewish community—as his poetic predecessors. But Rosenfeld quickly pushes beyond them. As he shifts his poetic attention and allegiance to the working class and their battle with the bosses of industry, he begins to politicize the form and rhetoric of the exhortative poem. Unlike the *maskilim* (proponents of the Jewish Enlightenment), Rosenfeld does not call on his readers to shed their Jewish way of life and embrace European culture. Rather, he implores them to cast off the shackles of manual labor and, through a workers' revolution, destroy the capitalist system.

The distance between these two positions illuminates a crucial difference in their approaches to language. The *maskilim* chose Yiddish as a literary vehicle with great deliberation and regret. For these writers, the Eastern European Jewish vernacular was a "crippled" tongue, more a *zhargon* (jargon) than a full-fledged language. They considered Yiddish a linguistic barrier, which prevented Jews not only from appreciating European culture and education but also from integrating into European society. Ideally, the *maskilim* preferred to write their appeals to the Jewish people in other languages, particularly Hebrew, which had a long and venerable literary tradition. But the audience they wished to reach did not, for the most part, speak or read Hebrew, so the *haskala* writers turned to Yiddish. Although they considered it a vulgar, impure, and base vehicle, these authors felt they had no other choice but to write in Yiddish if they were going to communicate successfully with Jewish readers. They intended Yiddish to be a temporary linguistic vehicle, which they would discard as Jews learned to read foreign languages such as German and Russian.[1]

Sweatshop poets shared the ideological, didactic, and universalist leanings of their *haskala* predecessors, but not their disdain for the Yiddish language. Despite the persistent stigma attached to the Eastern European Jewish vernacular, they chose to write in their mother tongue for their largely uneducated Jewish readers, who knew only Yiddish. Rosenfeld went even further in his mature Sweatshop poetry: he aimed to enrich literary Yiddish, whose lexicon he would expand in two innovative ways. First, he would employ common figurative language in uniquely novel ways. Second, he would make extended use of *daytshmerish* (Germanized) words and phrases. These expressions—borrowed from New High German—were commonplace in nineteenth-century Yiddish literature, and Rosenfeld applied them to his poems with great skill.

Because sentimental-melodramatic poetry deals with serious existential, ethical, and moral matters, it must possess an elevated tone. At the same time, straightforward, uncomplicated communication between poet and reader is indispensable; the language of these works must be simple—understood clearly at first glance. Moreover, both the syntax of the poetry and its relationship to the prosody that carries it must also so be simple, though still highly artistic. Rosenfeld's mature Sweatshop poetry more than fulfills these requirements; he casts the semantic meaning of his poems in such a way that syntax dovetails nicely with prosody.

Because the speaker's message is important and pressing, the sentimental-melodramatic poet relies heavily on incrementalized repetition, having the speaker often repeat a word, phrase, or sentence throughout a line, stanza, or poem. The poet uses this type of repetition to express the emotional level of the speaker and to heighten or even ceremonialize the tone and level of the poem—making the poem's message more important through the elevation of register and the dramatization of mood, rather than through additional semantic contents.

The language of the sentimental-melodramatic model also deals with stark oppositions that the poet employs to express the belief that life is made up of diametrically opposing forces, the speaker or interlocutor of the poem representing one of these forces. These oppositions are connected to another common feature of this model, namely, the use of hyperbole. Because the world represented in these poems has such an immediate and extreme nature, language must reflect this condition.

The figurative language of the sentimental-melodramatic poem—like its style in general—is almost always straightforward. Furthermore, this model relies on metaphors drawn from a repertoire of stock figurative language to which the poet consistently turns. In his mature Sweatshop poems, Rosenfeld not only uses the same metaphors repeatedly, but he exploits them, wringing them of their full emotional potential. In doing so, he brings new meaning to metaphors overused and even threadbare in modern Yiddish poetry, particularly in the early Sweatshop poems. For example, and not surprisingly, the metaphor to which the poet most often turns in his sentimental-melodramatic poems is the tear. As it does for the late-nineteenth-century longing-for-Zion Hebrew poetry of Hibbat Zion, the tear defines the metaphoric landscape of Rosenfeld's mature Sweatshop poetry.

In "A trer afn ayzn" (A Tear on the Iron), Rosenfeld provides a clear example of this metaphor, but not before first using the tear in several other rhetorical and figurative ways. In the poem's first two stanzas, the poet establishes the setting common to most of his proletarian poetry:

> O, kalt un finster iz di shap!
> Ikh halt dem ayzn, shtey un klap!
> Mayn herts iz shvakh, ikh krekhts un hust;
> es heybt zikh koym mayn kranke brust.
>
> Ikh krekhts un hust un pres un kler,
> mayn oyg vert faykht, es falt a trer,
> der ayzn glit: dos trerl mayn
> dos kokht un kokht un zidt nit ayn. (14)
>
> [Oh cold and dark is the shop!
> I hold the iron, stand and strike!
> My heart is weak, I moan and cough,
> my sick chest barely heaves.
>
> I moan and cough and press and think,
> my eye dampens, a tear falls,
> the iron glows: my little tear
> it boils and boils and does not evaporate.]

The tear as synecdoche is a figure of primary importance in sentimental literature and Rosenfeld employs it in a straightforward manner to represent the sadness of the ailing, toiling immigrant worker. The poet focuses on the speaker-protagonist's spiritual condition, which turns on the word *kler* (think). The speaker works, moans, and coughs, but it is his act of reflection that produces the tear. Yet Rosenfeld pushes beyond the obvious metaphoric meaning of the tear, transforming it into a symbol of mythical proportions. The narrative slows down, and this single teardrop becomes the focus of the entire poem. To emphasize the unusual quality of the tear, the poet makes a clear reference to a similar paradox, the burning bush before which Moses stood (Exodus 3:2), the supernatural bush that burned, yet was not consumed. The speaker is instantly affected by this event, and this unnatural phenomenon causes him to pause from his work:

> Ikh fil keyn kraft, es iz farvent;
> der ayzn falt mir fun di hent,
> un dokh der trer, der heyser trer,
> der trer, der trer, kokht mer un mer. (14)

> [I have no more strength, it's all been used;
> the iron falls from my hand,
> and still the tear, the hot tear,
> the tear, the tear, boils more and more.]

As the speaker stands and watches his lone tear, its resilience amazes him. Against the force of the hot iron it does not evaporate—as one would expect—but continues to seethe. Rosenfeld's use of alliteration here serves to emphasize the centrality of this figure, as he repeats the final, masculine rhyme of *er*: "un dokh der trer, der heyser trer, / der trer, der trer, kokht mer un mer."

Time is now greatly decelerated—if not completely stopped—and, in an elevation of rhetoric and style typical of the sentimental mode, the protagonist apostrophizes the individual tear, asking of it several questions:

Es roysht mayn kop, es brekht mayn herts;
ikh freg mit vey, ikh freg mit shmerts:
"O, zog, mayn fraynd in noyt un payn,
o, trer, farvos zidstu nit ayn?

"O, shtumer trer, o, shtume shprakh!
Zog, hob ikh dayne nokh a sakh?
Tsi du bist shoyn der letster haynt,
fun ale mayne heyse fraynt?

"Bist efsher gor a kuriyer,
zogst on mir, az es kumen mer?
Ikh volt es velen visn, zog:
ven endikt zikh der groyser klog?" (14–15)

[My head whirls, my heart breaks;
I ask in sorrow, I ask in suffering:
"Oh, tell me, my friend in need and pain,
oh, tear, why don't you evaporate?

"Oh, silent tear, oh, silent speech!
Tell me, do I have many more of you?
Or are you the last today,
of all my hot friends?

"Perhaps you are a messenger,
telling me that more are coming?
I would like to know, tell me:
When will this great sorrow end?"]

The speaker thus personifies the tear—as well as the future tears he anticipates—and, through the use of double meaning, transforms the synecdoche into a metaphor. Calling these anticipated tears "heyse fraynt" (warm friends), Rosenfeld employs the elaborate form of periphrasis common in sentimental literature, but, in an artistic manner, plays upon the literal and metaphorical meanings of *heys*. On the one hand, the tears are literally hot when they hit the iron, but the expression *heyse fraynt* in Yiddish also denotes close, loyal friendship. This tear then not only represents the great sadness in the life of the speaker, a sadness that is common to the lives of immigrant shop workers in general, but also serves as a metaphor for Rosenfeld's poems. The tear—like the sweatshop poem itself—is a product of sad reflection upon a life of suffering. The speaker produces the tear the same way the poet produces a poem. This tear, however, is special. Unlike an average tear, which would quickly, almost instantly evaporate after coming into contact with a hot iron, this tear not only resists the destructive power of the iron, but also appropriates its heat and strength. The tear, then is a poetic creation of lasting value and not only the poem itself, but a prophetic-poetic vision. By referring to the burning bush before which Moses stood when God informed him of his mission to lead the children of Israel out of Egypt, Rosenfeld points to the speaker-poet's calling. The metaphor now becomes a symbol; like the burning bush, the mythical tear is pregnant with additional meanings and the lonely sweatshop press operator is not just a simple worker, but a poet experiencing an epiphany. The speaker's prophecy, however, concludes on an ambivalent note:

> Ikh volt gefregt nokh mer un mer,
> bam umru, ba dem vildn trer,
> do hobn zikh derlangt a gos
> gor trern, trern on a mos
> un ikh hob shoyn farshtanen glaykh,
> az tif iz nokh der trern taykh. (15)

> [I would have liked to asked more and more,

of the unrest, of the wild tear,
and then a stream came forth
of tears, an unlimited amount of tears
and I quickly understood,
that the river of tears is still deep.]

The single tear responds spontaneously to the questions that
the speaker has posed in the previous stanzas. A stream of "unlimited" tears pours forth and this final note reveals both sides of the
metaphor. Poetic inspiration and productivity are definitely abundant, but so too is the great sadness in the life of the immigrant
worker.

Rosenfeld engages the idea of the tear as a metaphor not only
for the suffering of the individual, but also for poetry, in another of
his central Sweatshop poems, "Der trern miliyoner" (The Teardrop Millionaire):

O, nit keyn goldner kamerton
shtimt on mayn kel tsum zingn,
es ken der vunk fun oybn on
mayn shtim nit makhn klingn;
dem shklavs a krekhts, ven er iz mid
nor vekt in mir di lider,
un mit a flam lebt uf mayn lid,
far mayne or'me brider. (7)

[Oh, no golden tuning fork
tunes my throat to sing,
the wink from up above
does not make my voice ring;
only the slave's groan, when he is tired
wakes in me the poems,
and with a flame my poem comes to life,
for my poor brothers.]

The sentimental-melodramatic speaker—again, a worker-poet—reveals that he does not receive his poetic inspiration from typical, elevated sources, but rather locates his muse in the suffering, working masses, the "poor brothers" with whom he is intrinsically bound. They not only inspire him, as he states in the second stanza, but also represent his primary audience. Yet, how can they repay him for his poems, his labor? The speaker responds to his own question:

> Zey tsoln trern far a trer,
> dos alles, vos zey konen:
> Ikh bin a trern-miliyoner
> un veyn af di milyonen. (7)

> [They pay with tears for a tear,
> that is all they can afford:
> I am a tear millionaire
> and lament the millions.]

The poet here pushes the figure of the tear beyond a clever metaphor for his own poetry and creates a completely new idea in Yiddish poetry. In the poem's title—identical to its penultimate line—Rosenfeld uses logical opposition to establish an oxymoron. He does not symbolize sadness through the expected use of hyperbole common in sentimental poetry—such as the well-wrought "vale of tears" or "sea of tears"—but rather imbues it with complexity by adding a strong dose of irony. The poem's title and central image highlight the great ambivalence the speaker feels in his role as a poet, an ambivalence Rosenfeld first suggests in "A Tear on the Iron." On the one hand, the speaker is a poet with abundant tears and, therefore, abundant inspiration. On the other hand, however, he is a tremendously sad person who sheds "millions" of tears, and his only remuneration from his audience is more of the same. The speaker in "The Teardrop Millionaire" laments the thankless task in which he grows rich not in money, but in tears, thereby increasing not his personal wealth, but rather, his sadness. In "Der bleykher apreytor" (The Pale Operator), the protagonist of the poem also spills drops of liquid. In this case, however, it is the sweat that results from his manual labor:

Dokh faln di tropns keseyder,
fun ufgang biz untergang shpet,
un zapn zikh ayn in di kleyder,
un trinkn zikh ayn in di net. (12–13)

[The drops constantly fall,
from sunrise until well after sunset,
and are absorbed in the clothing,
and drown in the seams.]

Unlike the mythical "Tear on the Iron," which burns without evaporating, or the lasting, countless tears of "The Teardrop Millionaire," the sweat of "The Pale Operator," which falls from the worker and immediately disappears into his product acts as a synecdoche for the poem's protagonist. The ephemeral nature of this perspiration highlights its nondescriptiveness, which, for the speaker of the poem, represents the generic and exchangeable nature of the subject's entire being. Rosenfeld alludes to this connection throughout the poem, but states his point most clearly in the final stanza. In response to his own question as to how long the operator's sad and difficult life will last, the speaker states:

O, shver, zeyer shver dos tsu zogn,
dokh eyns iz bavust un basheyt:
ven im vet di arbet dershlogn,
zitst teykef a tsveyter un neyt. (13)

[It is hard, very hard to say,
but one thing is for certain:
when labor finally finishes him off,
someone else will take his place and sew.]

Just as the operator's sweat disappears unnoticed into his product, so too does he disappear easily into the capitalist machine. In the sweatshops of the Lower East Side, the lives of immigrant workers are as expendable—and as unnoticeable—as drops of sweat. The Pale Operator thus becomes a metaphor for the immigrant-worker experience, representing the sad and passing nature of this life.

Another metaphor Rosenfeld employs in his Sweatshop poetry is that of war, which earlier Yiddish poets such as Bovshover, Edelshtat, and Vinchevsky often used in their works. In his mature Sweatshop poems, however, the poet makes uncommon use of this common metaphor, endowing it with a new significance that reflects his pessimism. For Rosenfeld's contemporaries, the language of war was essential to their political beliefs because in their opinion *kamf* (struggle) was the natural state that existed between the upper and lower classes. These poets needed imagery that would illustrate and intensify this situation. In his earlier works, Rosenfeld uses the metaphors of war and battle in this bombastic and optimistic manner to incite his readers to revolt against the capitalist system. When, however, his worldview darkens, the poet employs this language in a correspondingly despondent manner.

Rosenfeld refers, for example, in the longer of his two poems entitled "The Sweatshop," to the workshop as a "shlakhtfeld" (battlefield) and "kamf-plats" (place of struggle). In other poems, he uses verbs such as "kemfn" (struggle), "shtraytn" (fight), and "yogn" (chase) as metaphors for shop work. In "The Pale Operator," the central figure "kemft mitn royen mashin" (struggles with the raw machine) and in "Tsu der gelibter" (To My Loved One) the shop worker explains that "do hersht der harter kamf far broyt" (here, the difficult struggle for bread rules). Unlike the earlier heroes of Sweatshop poetry who fight for political causes, these figures do not wage large, abstract battles, but rather, struggle in the simple, personal battle to earn a living. They do not "fight" the bosses for freedom or revolution, but rather, clash with the machines, simply to provide for themselves and their families. This subversion of the figurative language of war reflects Rosenfeld's disillusionment. Instead of appropriating his poetic protagonists for political causes, the poet instead focuses on the practical, everyday battles of the immigrant shop workers who are more interested in feeding their families than engaging in interclass warfare.

The poet also makes sustained use of the metaphor of slavery to demonstrate his pessimism. As opposed to his earlier works, as well as those of his contemporary Sweatshop poets, in which these writers, relying heavily on the imagery of heroism and battle, refer optimistically to the working masses as "soldiers" or "fighters," the mature Rosenfeld calls them "slaves" and their task—as he states, for instance, in "Despair"—"slavery." In "The Teardrop Millionaire," the speaker-poet finds his inspiration in the pain of his fellow worker, "dem shklavs a krekhts" (the slave's moan); in "In the Shop and at Home," the protagonist complains that at work he is "gebundn" (bound); and in "Mayn ruhe plats" (My Resting Place), the poet laments: "A shklav bin ikh vu keytn klingn" (I am a slave where chains clang).

By referring to himself and his "brothers" in these terms, the speaker-worker-poet in "My Resting Place"—like many of Rosenfeld's other similarly identified speakers—points to the writer's pessimism. In addition, the poet's use of extreme figurative language, in this case that of slavery, leads to Rosenfeld's complementary use of rhetorical figures. "My Resting Place," like several of Rosenfeld's other shop works, is based on oppositions:

Nit zukh mikh, vu di foygl zingn!
Gefinst mikh dortn nit mayn shats;
a shklav bin ikh vu keytn klingn,
dortn iz mayn ruhe plats. (29)

[Do not look for me where birds sing!
You will not find me there my dear;
I am a slave where chains clang,
there is my rest place.]

Here the poet employs litotes, a common rhetorical figure that begins many Russian epics.[2] Instead of giving a straightforward definition of a concept, this device explains one idea by offering the negative meaning of its contrary idea; the speaker does not tell us where he is, but rather, where he is not. In "My Resting Place," this device heralds the basic structure of the entire poem in which Rosenfeld focuses on the presence of oppositions in the life of the shop worker. Not only are the natural and unnatural settings of the first and third lines opposite, but they also each represent an extreme situation. Nature is not merely a passive calm field, but rather a place where birds actively sing. Conversely, the shop is not simply a boring or stale environment, but a place where the physical bonds of labor imprison the speaker who likens himself to a slave. Because, as Peter Brooks states in his study of melodrama, the raison d'être and chief task of this mode is nothing less than the full disclosure of "basic ethical and psychic truths," its rhetoric must be necessarily elevated to represent properly the seriousness of its cause.[3] Rosenfeld's stylistic use of hyperbole and elevated poetic speech thus are not mere rhetorical devices but are invested with much significance.

There are numerous examples of Rosenfeld's use of hyperbole and exaggeration throughout his oeuvre. The subject of "The Teardrop Millionaire," for example, operates not in scores, hundreds, or even thousands, but in millions of tears; the speaker in "A Tear on the Iron" deals in "an unlimited amount of tears"; and when the protagonist-speaker of "My Boy" watches his boy sleep, he feels that "the whole world is mine." In these examples, Rosenfeld employs heightened language to underscore his main message, namely, that the themes of his poems reflect the deep seriousness and sadness of the human condition.

Another of Rosenfeld's common figures of speech is the rhetorical question. In the first verse of "Despair," the speaker asks:

> O, darf men nit ruen khotsh eyn tog in vokh,
> a tog mer nit fray zayn fun shreklekhn yokh?
> Fargesn dem bos, dem farbisenem mruk,
> zayn finstere mine, zayn shreklekhn kuk,
> fargesn di shap un dem forman's geshrey,
> fargesn di knekhtshaft, fargesn dem vey,
> "fargesn zikh vilstu un ruen dertsu?
> nit zorg zikh, ot bald vestu geyn in dayn ru!" (19)

> [Must one not rest even one day of the week,
> to be free at least one day from the dreadful yoke?
> To forget the boss, the embittered grumbler,
> his dark face, his frightening look,
> to forget the shop and the foreman's shouting,
> to forget slavery, to forget woe,
> "you wish to forget yourself and be rested as well?
> Do not worry, you will soon go to your rest!"]

Here the poet poses a rhetorical question to which the answer seems obvious and then subverts it. In the last two lines of this stanza, and in the subsequent stanzas of this poem, Rosenfeld introduces a second poetic voice, which mocks the first through the use of double meaning and bitter irony that slips into sarcasm.

The first speaker in "Despair" attempts to convince his readers of his fair-mindedness. Unlike earlier proletarian poetry, the worker here does not call for a communist revolution or the termination of the entire capitalist system; accepting his fate as a cog in the wheel of "slavery," he wants something much more immediate and reasonable: "one day of the week" to "forget" work. To underscore the modesty of this request, Rosenfeld repeats the word "fargesn" (to forget) four times. The second voice, however, enters in the last lines of the stanza and, in a sinister and sarcastic tone, assures the worker that the only rest he will ever earn is the final and permanent rest of death.

Rosenfeld further expanded literary Yiddish with his extended use of *daytshmerish*.[4] As he does with figurative language, Rosenfeld takes a prevalent means of contemporary poetic expression and imbues with new significance. Although used by many nineteenth—and early-twentieth-century Yiddish writers of both "high" and "low" literary status' in their poetry and prose, *daytshmerish*—the borrowing of lexical elements from New High German (NHG)[5] and their incorporation into the literary language of modern Yiddish, *moderne yidishe kulturshprakh* (Modern Yiddish Cultural Language; MYCL)—'was vilified 'by many critics. Indeed, it became a central issue of contention in Yiddish linguistic and literary studies.

Max Weinreich, one of the leading Yiddish scholars of the past century and a man widely regarded as the dean of Yiddish studies, is perhaps the best representative of the anti-*daytshmerish* camp. In his influential article, appropriately and simply entitled *"Daytshmerish* Will Not Do," Weinreich summarizes his view on this issue: "The bottom line: There is no greater enemy of a correct, tasteful, exact, Jewish General-Yiddish than *daytshmerish*. The natural tendency in the development of the language of the Ashkenazi Jews was, from the beginning, the moving away from German toward original creation; and we see this especially clearly in the branch of Yiddish that withstood the storms—Eastern European Yiddish. But this natural tendency was spoiled through streams of *daytshmerish*, which inundated it from various sides."[6] The Yiddishism inherent in this view is also evident in the definition that Mordkhe Shekhter, a contemporary Yiddish linguist, offers: *"Daytshmerizmn* [Germanisms] are the NHG words and forms which were imported [into the MYCL], despite the fact that we already had our own resources, or could have managed with neologisms formed from our own resources."[7] In lexical terms, Germanisms *(daytshmerizmn)* are NHG words used by speakers or writers of the Eastern European Jewish vernacular that, in the Yiddishist opinion, should be avoided wherever there are MYCL equivalents.

In a 1991 essay, the linguistic scholar Hirshe-Dovid Kats argues that the *"daytshmerish* scare is over."[8] Kats's article is, in large part, a critique of the well-known and universally used *Modern English-Yiddish, Yiddish-English Dictionary*, compiled by Uriel Weinreich, Max Weinreich's son and a leading scholar in his own right.[9] In particular, Kats criticizes the criteria that Weinreich uses to disqualify certain words from inclusion in the Yiddish vocabulary. Kats argues democratically that Yiddish speakers and writers should decide for themselves which words are acceptable and which not. His advice is simple: "If you do not like a certain word, then do not use it."[10] For Kats, NHG words offer variety to the writer of Yiddish and increase the richness of the language. He subsequently lists several New High German words that were incorporated into the Modern Yiddish Cultural Language in the nineteenth century—after the traditional cutoff point of admissibility, according to traditional Yiddishist linguists—which today are seen as perfectly acceptable Yiddish terms: *arbeter* (worker), *literatur* (literature), *frage* (question), *tsaytung* (newspaper), and *shprakh* (language).

Kats has no problem enriching the Modern Yiddish Cultural

Language with New High German. Indeed, like-minded contemporary readers may wonder why there is such resistance to New High German, not only among scholars, but also among many speakers and readers of Yiddish. Why has there been no similar resistance to the inclusion of Slavic, Hebrew-Aramaic, or Romance-language components in the Modern Yiddish Cultural Language? Why do mainstream Yiddishists deem it acceptable to use an "internationalism"—a word borrowed from one of the other source languages—to create a neologism, but not a word borrowed from NHG?

The Yiddishist perspective argues that, as a result of "natural" forces, Yiddish moved away from German, the language that constitutes the largest linguistic component of the Jewish vernacular. This argument seems to imply that Yiddish evolved "naturally" as Ashkenazi Jews migrated from the upper Rhine valley—the accepted birthplace of the language—across the Germanic lands, to Eastern Europe. In other words, the vernacular evolved with exposure to new local languages as Yiddish-speaking Jews moved east from Germany through Poland to Russia. Traditional Yiddishists consider the foreign influences of Polish, Russian, and other host languages acceptable, yet they resist the "infiltration" of *daytshmerish* as an "unnatural" phenomenon.

Yiddishist scholars such as Weinreich and Mordkhe Shekhter argue that seventeenth-century Eastern European Jewish merchants first imported these words and phrases when they traveled to Prussia for business and then returned home with new German expressions, which they wielded as status symbols. Early proponents of the *haskala,* many of whom were enthusiasts of the widely admired German language and culture, included many Germanisms in their written works. Foremost among these *maskilim* was the prolific A. M. Dik. Although Yiddish writers such as Dik attempted to introduce NHG to the Yiddish reading audience as an educational tool, later writers used Germanisms,' according to

Shekhter, to boast of their erudition and education, as did the earlier merchants. An example of a writer who used *daytshmerish* in this manner is Shomer (N. M. Shaykevitsh), the popular author of *shund* (popular, sensationalistic "trash") novels.[11] Yiddishist scholars consider these attempts to incorporate New High German into the Modern Yiddish Cultural Language as contrived and unnatural because the new words and expressions of NHG origin did not fill lexical needs.

Kats argues convincingly, however, that many words of NHG extraction did indeed fill lexical gaps and that it is thus important to ask why Yiddishists objected so to these specific borrowings. Indeed, beginning at the turn of the twentieth century, there was a move to nationalize Yiddish; in 1908, the Chernovitz Conference declared Yiddish to be a national language of the Jewish people. For their part, Yiddishists shunned *daytshmerish* largely because it emerged from the critical view of Jewish life in Europe expressed by the proponents of the *haskala*. But from a postideological perspective, *daytshmerish* must be understood and treated as a legitimate social phenomenon of merging societies.

One of the central complaints leveled at Rosenfeld is that his poetry is filled with too much *daytshmerish*. Nokhem Borekh Minkov, however, explains in the introduction to his seminal work *Pioneers of Yiddish Poetry in America,* that *daytshmerish* played an important role in American Yiddish poetry because it gave these works an elevated, more poetic feel. For example, explaining the difference in nuance between New High German *mond* (moon) and the MYCL *levone* (moon), he writes: "*Levone* was clearly an ordinary, simple word. However, *mond*—this was something different. This word was new. Moreover, it possessed an elevated, lyrical key. When the young man said to the young woman: 'You are as beautiful as the *mond*,' she became excited and overwhelmed. And *vare libe* ["true love" in NHG] meant more than *emese libe* ["true love" in MYCL]."[12] Minkov holds that the NHG borrowings filled emotional, social, and aesthetic needs. In addition, he argues that many Yiddish readers of this era accepted NHG elements, even though branded as *daytshmerish*, as lyrical, literary, and elevated.

Minkov's argument was brave and somewhat radical for its time. In the 1950s, his opinions flew in the face of the Yiddishist establishment. The Holocaust had decimated their ranks and only strengthened the anti-German resolve of the survivors. During the postwar period, leading scholars such as Max Weinreich turned even further away from NHG elements in Yiddish.

When Morris Rosenfeld began his career in the 1880s, the use of *daytshmerish* was prevalent in Yiddish literature and in the fledgling Yiddish press, which, particularly in America, was almost the only outlet for Yiddish poetry. Many Yiddish writers besides A. M. Dik and Shomer used' *daytshmerish* in their works, particularly the poets—in Europe, Y. L. Peretz, Shimen Frug, and H. N. Bialik; in America, Yoysef Bovshover, Dovid Edelshtat, and Morris Vinchevsky. Like Rosenfeld, these poets felt that Yiddish in itself was not a totally suitable vehicle for lyrical expression; they used *daytshmerish* to embellish the language.

In "Fun dikhter tsum folk" (From the Poet to the People), the introduction to his *Shriftn,* Rosenfeld apologizes to his readers, explaining that, because he has great difficulty communicating his feelings in prose, he will do so in a poem instead. In the third stanza, he quotes an imaginary detractor who questions his "dream" of writing Yiddish poetry:

> Vi ken a toyter bodn trogn flantsn?
> Vi kumt a vilde shprakh tsu sheyne lider?
> Vi ken der proster shteyn vi dimant glantsn?
> Vos dult er undz mit zayn fantaziye vider? (xviii)

> [How can a dead terrain sustain plants?

What does a wild language have to do with beautiful poems?
How can the coarse stone shine like a diamond?
Why does he keep annoying us with his fantasy?]

In poetic form, Rosenfeld expresses his own anxieties about the appropriateness of writing poetry in Yiddish. As Dan Miron explains in *A Traveler Disguised*, Yiddish, derisively referred to as "zhargon," was not at all the logical choice for the early authors of modern Yiddish literature. Indeed, most Yiddish authors began their literary careers in a different language, often Hebrew.[13] Unlike the previous generation of Yiddish poets, who were proponents of the *haskala*, however, Rosenfeld did not treat Yiddish "as Caliban," to use Miron's phrase. Rather, the poet sought to expand the language and *daytshmerish* was one of the main vehicles he used to refine and poeticize the Jewish vernacular.

In Rosenfeld's poetry, *daytshmerish* functions in a number of ways. For example, in the longer of the two poems entitled "The Sweatshop," the poet uses several forms of the NHG word *shtunde* (hour; in MYCL, *sho*). This word is central to the poem, which, as we saw in the previous chapter of this study, accuses time—a metaphor for historical forces—of oppressing the workers. In the second stanza, the speaker laments the passing of too much time spent working: "Es shvindn sekundn, minutn un shtundn, / gor zegel-shnel flien di nekht mit di teg" (8). [Disappearing are the seconds, minutes, and hours, / sailing, flying, go the nights and days.]

The word "shtundn" is important here not only because it represents an increase in time increments, from seconds to minutes to hours, but also because of the internal rhyme of "undn." Repeated rhyme in this work acts as a vehicle for the monotony of the shop, something that the poet would not have created as successfully had he relied upon the MYCL. Rosenfeld uses the singular NHG form *shtunde* twice and the plural *shtundn* twice. But it is his additional usage of this word that is most interesting. In the fifth stanza, the poet describes a brief quiet moment in the workday:

> Nor dan, ven siz shtiler der vilder getuml,
> avek iz der mayster in mitog-tsayt shtund,
> dan fangn on in kop tsu togn,
> in hartsn tsu tsiyen,—ikh fil dan mayn vund (9)

> [But then, when the wild racket quiets down,
> the boss is away during the lunch-time hour,
> then day begins dawning in my head,
> pulling on my heart,—I then feel my wound]

Here Rosenfeld does not use the singular *shtunde,* as might be expected, but rather, innovatively creates a Yiddish neologism, *shtund,* to satisfy both rhyme and meter. The poet does not merely borrow from NHG, but he also adapts his borrowings and, in doing so, expands the vocabulary of modern Yiddish poetry.

Another poem in which Rosenfeld uses NHG words to satisfy poetic functions is "My Boy." In lamenting that he hardly gets to spend any time with his son, the speaker-father states:

> Nor zeltn, zeltn ze ikh im,
> mayn sheynem, ven er vakht,
> ikh tref im imer shlofndik,
> ikh ze im nor ba nakht (16)

> [But seldom, seldom do I see him,
> my beautiful one, when he is awake,
> I find him always sleeping,
> I see him only at night]

Uriel Weinreich includes this poem in his *College Yiddish,*[14] the basic textbook for beginning and intermediate Yiddish language study. Weinreich, however, in the above cited verse, switches "imer" to "tomid," the more acceptable Hebrew-element alternative for "always," and this textual emendation alters the entire feel of the stanza. Rosenfeld's use of alliteration is key to stressing the constancy of the father's sadness; "im imer" (him always) sounds like "imer imer" (always always), which underscores the fact that, due to his punishing work schedule, the father never interacts with his son while the boy is awake. By switching "imer" to "tomid," to create a more "Yiddish" stanza—according to Yiddishist standards—Weinreich weakens the overall effect of the poet's words and evocations.

As Minkov correctly asserts, the evocative nature of *daytshmerish* finds extended expression in Yiddish literature. This evocative nature saturates one of Rosenfeld's best-known and widely anthologized poems, "Mayn ruhe plats" (My Rest Place):

Nit zukh mikh vu di mirtn grinen!
Gefinst mikh dortn nit, mayn shats;
vu lebns velkn ba mashinen,
dortn iz mayn ruhe plats.

Nit zukh mikh, vu di foygl zingn!
Gefinst mikh dortn nit, mayn shats;
a shklav bin ikh vu keytn klingn,
dortn iz mayn ruhe plats.

Nit zukh mikh, vu fantonen shpritsn!
Gefinst mikh dortn nit, mayn shats;
vu trern rinen, tseyner kritsn,
dortn iz mayn ruhe plats.

Un libstu mikh mit vare libe,
to kum tsu mir, mayn guter shats!
Un heyter uf mayn herts di tribe,

un makh mir zis mayn ruhe plats (29)

[Do not look for me, where myrtles grow!
You will not find me there, my dear;
where lives wither at machines,
there is my rest place.

Do not look for me where the birds sing!
You will not find me there, my dear;
a slave am I where chains clang,
there is my rest place.

Do not look for me where fountains spray
You will not find me there, my dear;
where tears run, teeth grind,
there is my rest place.

And if you love me with true love,
then come to me my good dear!
And raise my sad heart,
and sweeten for me my rest place.]

    The NHG components are crucial to this poem; without them, the work would lose its full meaning. The title itself, which is the poem's central image, would not have the same thrust: the word "ruhe" (rest) must maintain its disyllabic German pronunciation not only to fit the meter of the poem (in the MYCL this title would be "Mayn ru plats"), but also to stress the elevated nature of the image. Specifically, Rosenfeld uses *daytshmerish* in this poem to stress the gap between NHG language and the sophisticated European culture it represents, and the painful and unredeemable life of the shop. The speaker of the poem says that you will not find him in genteel places where fountains spray, but rather in the slavish and oppressive environment of the shop. The poet invokes typical Germanized phrases such as "mayn shats" (my dear) and "vare libe" (true love) to emphasize both the literal and metaphorical distances between these two different environments.

While Rosenfeld indeed uses *daytshmerish* to create a feeling of elevated and sophisticated language, it also serves a second, more subversive purpose in "My Resting Place." The language undermines itself by highlighting the contrast between form and content, between language and idea. *Daytshmerish* represents what is beautiful and poetic, yet artificial and unattainable, in contrast to the real life of the speaker, which is toil and death in the shop.

Another example of Rosenfeld's ironic use of *daytshmerish* is in the poem "Vuhin?" (Whither?):

Vuhin, vuhin, du sheynes kind,
zo shpet ba nakht shpatsirn?
Aleyn durkh finsternish un kelt!
Un ales rut, es shvaygt di velt,
vuhin fort trogt es dikh der vint?
Du vest nokh dokh fariren!
Koym hot der tog dir nit gelakht,
vos ken dir helfn den di nakht?
Zi iz dokh shtum un toyb un blind!
Vuhin mit laykhtn zinen?
"Ikh gey fardinen!" (30–31)

[Whither, whither, you beautiful child,
are you walking so late at night?
Alone through darkness and cold!
And everything is at rest, the world is silent,
where is the wind carrying you?
You will yet go astray!
The day could hardly keep from mocking you,
how then can the night help?
It is, after all, deaf and dumb and blind!

Whither are you going so recklessly?

"I am going to earn a living!"]

The speaker addresses the working girl, using several Germanized expressions, such as "du sheynes kind" (you beautiful child), "zo shpet" (so late), "fariren" (go astray) and "mit laykhtn zinen" (so recklessly). Rosenfeld uses this language to represent the false gentility of the speaker, someone who seems not to share in the girl's struggle for daily bread. The poet emphasizes the distance between the two through language. Ultimately, in response to the speaker's lengthy question, which is couched in Germanized, and thus artificially refined, speech, the girl responds in plain and simple Yiddish: "Ikh gey fardinen" (I am going to earn a living).

Reading Rosenfeld's poetry from a Yiddishist perspective, it is indeed tempting to replace certain New High German words with their counterparts in the general MYCL. The canon of modern Yiddish literature, as typified by its three classic writers—S. J. Abramovitch, Sholem Aleykhem, and Y. L. Peretz—is heavily based on the Yiddish *folkshprakh* (the language of the people). Rosenfeld might have expressed himself in a more "Yiddish" manner, but this would have produced very different results and compromised the core meaning of his poetry. Although the Yiddish *folkshprakh* indeed possesses unique and useful merits, Rosenfeld needed other means to portray reality in a sentimental-melodramatic manner and to express the artificial nature of literature.

Although Rosenfeld employs *daytshmerish* to stress the gap between genteel culture and the actual life of the immigrant shop worker, he, at the same time, unites these two worlds in an ambivalent manner in the microcosm of his poetry. He claims that, in real life, these two opposites never meet, but they appear together on his printed page. Still, it is evident that they do not meet here either. Indeed, in "My Resting Place," Rosenfeld sets these two worlds directly against each other. On a linguistic level, he reinforces this idea of separateness through his use of a Germanized Yiddish, a poetic language clearly distinct from the *heymish* (familiar, traditional vernacular) of his audience.

Rosenfeld's use of *daytshmerish,* then, forms part of his wider use of figurative language. Like his employment of metaphors in conjuring specific figurative associations, the poet's substitutive applications of *daytshmerizmn* fulfill these same needs. Germanized language, however, unlike his other forms of figurative language, was and, to some extent continues to be, politically charged. Rosenfeld utilizes *daytshmerish* not only to "elevate" his poetry, but also in a more interesting and significant manner, to highlight the great distance between the ideal of poetry and the narratives he relates. The result is a unique brand of Sweatshop poetry, in which the poet acknowledges this distance in unresolved oppositions.

Attacks on Rosenfeld and his contemporaries for using *daytshmerish* are anachronistic. The critics who indulge in them ignore the fact that *daytshmerish* was simply part and parcel of the nineteenth—and early-twentieth-century Yiddish literary language. Grounded in the beliefs of the *haskala,* these poets, novelists, and short story writers felt that German was the normative language of culture and sought to elevate Yiddish by incorporating NHG elements into their literary works. In the case of sentimental-melodramatic poetry, where the judgments and statements made by the poet must be both elevated and universal, *daytshmerish* was a natural and necessary choice for Yiddish poets. Because the sentimental-melodramatic poet must, first and foremost, be easily understood by his readers, his language must be simple. But, by the conventions of the model, his language must never be conversational or idiomatic. Rosenfeld thus turned to common Germanisms to elevate his poetry without alienating his audience.

5

The Jewish Representative

Beginning in the 1870s, a new Yiddish literature began to emerge in America and, by the late 1880s—due in no small part to the rapidly expanding, radical Yiddish press—a new school of poetry had emerged. Soon to be called the "Sweatshop poets," these writers composed stirring, propagandistic poetry in which they attempted to convince their working-class audience to embrace ideologies such as socialism, communism, and anarchism. Although there were scores of such poets, many of them prolific and influential, the history of Yiddish literature has preserved only four— Yoysef Bovshover, Dovid Edelshtat, Morris Vinchevsky, and Morris Rosenfeld. Most literary studies and anthologies have given scant attention to these writers, acknowledging their work for its historical significance, but rarely, if at all, for its aesthetic merits.

Although they tended to dismiss the other three enduring Sweatshop poets as premodern authors of subliterary poetry, many critics and readers embraced Rosenfeld, not only as the most talented member of his literary generation, but also as the only representative of the school of Sweatshop poetry. Throughout the 1890s, as his poetic pessimism and despair grew, Rosenfeld's works increased in popularity, first among his immigrant shop worker audience in the United States, then, by the turn of the twentieth century, among audiences of many nations who read the poet in translation. As a result of his international success, Rosenfeld became the representative of the immigrant labor experience not only among his Yiddish audience, to whose collective life experience he gave voice, but also among audiences of widely differing linguistic and socioeconomic backgrounds. What distinguished Rosenfeld from his contemporaries? Why did his works resonate with his Yiddish readers more than those of his fellow Sweatshop poets? What was it about his works that aroused such wide interest in him? Why did Rosenfeld's detractors single him out from his fellow writers, focusing their attacks on Sweatshop poetry directly at him? Why was Rosenfeld chosen as the representative voice of Eastern European Jews?

Various audiences, both lay and professional, appropriated Rosenfeld throughout his career. Some celebrated the poet and his achievements; others vilified him and held up his work as an example of how little Yiddish poetry had achieved in America in the late nineteenth century. In their critical and theoretical writings, Di yunge barely acknowledge Bovshover, Edelshtat, or Vinchevsky, funneling their entire contempt for Sweatshop poetry into their attacks on Rosenfeld. Under the banner of "Art for art's sake," Di yunge considered Rosenfeld's poems as nothing more than expressions of his political ideologies and thus of little literary value. They minimized Rosenfeld's achievements and dismissed his wide appeal by pointing out that Rosenfeld's largely uneducated working-class readers were incapable of appreciating true poetry.

It is this appeal, however, that leads Yiddishist critics to laud the poet's accomplishments: they insist that the chief value of his poetry is that it represented the life of the Eastern European Jewish immigrant worker. These critics assign Rosenfeld especial poetic credibility because he lived the life he portrayed, emerging from the immigrant, working masses who served as his muse. For the Yiddishists, Rosenfeld may not have accomplished a great deal in aesthetic terms, but his portrayal of the first era of Eastern European Jewish immigration to America did much to develop the infant field of Yiddish literature and to advance the literary education of his immigrant audience. Moreover, the Yiddishist critics appreciated the fact that translations of Rosenfeld's works helped legitimize Yiddish among an international audience.

During the first decade of the twentieth century, this international audience attended Rosenfeld's public readings and purchased his books, many of which were published in multiple editions. Like no Yiddish writer before—and only a few after—Rosenfeld represented the life of the Eastern European Jew to the outside world. His sentimental and melodramatic accounts of the toil and suffering of the immigrant worker won him a large audience of European readers, many of whom learned of this world for the first time through Rosenfeld's poems. Here was a refined representative of a coarse world whose literature read very nicely in translation.

Once available in English, Rosenfeld found popularity and acceptance among Americans who could not read Yiddish; many were shocked to learn of the harsh lives of immigrants in their midst. A number of American literary critics viewed Rosenfeld's Sweatshop poems as interior portrayals of an exotic, semibarbaric world.

The German Jewish community, which included some of the wealthiest New York families, was markedly assimilated into American culture. Although they offered them patronage and charity, the German Jews encouraged their newly arrived immigrant brethren, who, for the most part, dressed, spoke, and looked like traditional Jews, to adopt New World ways. One notable example of these efforts was the daily *Di yidishe velt* (The Jewish World) founded in June 1902 by Louis Marshall for the express purpose of Americanizing Eastern European Jews. Rosenfeld published many of his poems here and served as the publication's literary editor. Encouraged by the poet's mass, transnational appeal,

Rosenfeld's wealthy, prominent patrons boasted of his achievements to the gentile world as a way to show that the Eastern European Jew was not an outsider, but an American who lived a life with which the poet's readers could empathize.

The poet was also tremendously popular within the community he portrayed. Indeed, as a member of this community, Rosenfeld mirrored its development through his Sweatshop poetry. As the newly arrived immigrants were exposed to the harsh labor conditions of the industrialized New World, a great protest arose among the workers. Rosenfeld, like his contemporary authors, expressed this outrage in the pages of the radical Yiddish press and demanded no less than a communist revolution that would topple the system and place the means of production in the hands of the workers. As this proletarian community soon realized that its idealistic goals were unattainable, many workers sunk into apathy and accepted their miserable lot in life. This dramatic shift in attitude clearly affected Rosenfeld's development as a poet, as demonstrated by the great pessimism and despair that saturated his mature Sweatshop poetry. The Yiddish-speaking, working-class audience identified with Rosenfeld's despair; his emotional poetry spoke to them.

Not only does Rosenfeld's Sweatshop poetry portray the life of the immigrant worker; more important, it paints a specific image of the Jew, one that resonated with many audiences. Unlike earlier Sweatshop poetry, which offered an heroic portrait of the Jew as a poetic-prophet warrior who represented the vanguard of the workers' movement, Rosenfeld's mature poems present men who are weak and suffering, men who lament their station in life in highly emotional terms and who accept their dark fates. Although it may seem puzzling that such an image of the Jew would appeal to the community it represented, there is no doubt that it greatly appealed to bourgeois audiences. Upper-class readers might take pleasure in sympathizing with the existential struggles of a factory worker, but they were much less likely to celebrate literature that called not only for their disenfranchisement, but also for their destruction, as did Rosenfeld's earlier, ideological poems. German Jews in America, some of them owners of New York City's sweatshops, found that such agitational poetry only served to alienate the Eastern European immigrants from their quiet form of intercession and integration. They much preferred the tamer, resigned image of the Eastern European Jew they found in Rosenfeld's mature Sweatshop poetry, especially as expressed in the refined English of his American translations.

Although critics differ on the specific values of Rosenfeld's poetry, almost all stress its authenticity. His proponents invoke it in praising the high quality of his poetry; his detractors consider it proof of the subpoetic quality of his work, his lack of literary sophistication and imagination. The issue of authenticity poses a real problem in analyzing Rosenfeld's works, as it does for the works of all writers portraying a given time and place. Because they cannot possibly represent every experience, writers must choose, and, more important, because the basic act of writing is interpretation, they must interpret. However many people on the Lower East Side and in other such American and European neighborhoods lived the life Rosenfeld describes in his poems, and however well-fashioned the body of that poetry, Rosenfeld's writings are the product of his own unique poetics of the immigrant experience.

The one aspect that almost all readers, whether bourgeois or working-class, could appreciate was the deep emotionalism of Rosenfeld's poetry, something he achieved through his use of sentimentalism and melodrama. Often the target of modernist sensibilities, literary melodrama enjoyed immense popularity throughout the history of modern and premodern literature and intrigued readers of almost all audiences. As both Peter Brooks and Robert Heilman explain, the typical structure of melodrama usually ends with the victory of virtue over evil. Many readers, particularly mass readers, took great satisfaction in seeing virtue rewarded and evil punished. But why did they also enjoy poems whose protagonists remained victims and whose prevaling mood was one of despair? What, then, was the appeal of Rosenfeld's darker, mature poetry?

Addressing this question, Heilman points to a singularity of feeling in melodrama, which he terms "monopathy." He argues that, as the dominant feature of melodrama, this emotional one-ness is the very quality that distinguishes it from tragedy. In tragedy, the self of the protagonist is flawed, divided against itelf, whereas in melodrama, the protagonist's self is united, whole—and this sense of wholeness is transmitted to the readers. More-over, the singular feeling of melodrama, whether of hope or of hopelessness, is satisfying in itself: in "the victor-victim polarity, there is no counterfeeling to offset the dominant emotion: the ap-proval of victory easily expands into self-congratulation, and the sadness for the defeated glides gently into the melancholy pleas-ures of self-pity."[1] Thus one of the strengths of melodrama's unity of feeling is that it draws readers into its emotional structure, caus-ing them to identify with the protagonist and, more crucially, to in-ternalize the protagonist's feelings.

Heilman argues further that the most appealing form of melo-drama is one in which the protagonist is not merely a victim, but innocent as well. This scenario clearly fits Rosenfeld's mature Sweatshop poems, in which protagonists are innocent victims of "the system," symbolized by manual labor and personified by the shop bosses. Rosenfeld employs words such as *gut* (good) and *reyn* (pure) to describe the victims, clearly underscoring their inno-cence. Rich or poor, Jewish or gentile, readers identified with these poetic protagonists, whose basic, existential struggles offered a singularity of emotion that satisfied both their literary and their psychological needs.

APPENDIX

NOTES

BIBLIOGRAPHY

APPENDIX

Chronological List of Works by Morris Rosenfeld

"Dos yor 1886." December 1886.

"Dos vign-lid." January 1887.

Di gloke: Folks lider und revolutsiyonere gedikhte. 1888.

"Der veker der frayheyt." June 1888.

"Di revolutsiyon." July 1888.

"Biz danen!"; "Un alzo"; "Vi lang nokh?" September 1888.

Di blumenkete: A zamlung fun farshidene folks lider un poeziyen. 1890.

Poeziyen un lider. Ershter teyl: Natsiyonele lider. 1893.

"In shap"; "Mayn yingele." January 1893.

Lider bukh: Ershter teyl. 1897.

Gezamlte lider. 1904.

Geklibene lider. 1905.

Heinrich Heine: Daytshland's grester liriker. 1906.

Yehuda halevi: Der grester hebreyisher dikhter. 1907.

Shriftn fun Moris Rozenfeld. 1908–10.

Gevelte shriftn. 1912.

Dos bukh fun libe. 1914.

Grine tsores un andere shriftn. 1919.

Moris Rozenfelds briv. 1955.

Notes

1. The First Yiddish Best Seller

1. Morris Rosenfeld, *Moris Rozenfelds briv,* ed. Yekhezkel Lifshitz (Buenos Aires: YIVO, 1955), 25–28. Rosenfeld's collected letters (henceforth *MRb*), as well as his archive at the YIVO, serve as the two main sources for his biography because of the lack of a scholarly biographical study of the poet. The only two full-length studies of the author are both problematic. The first is a fictionalized retelling of the poet's life by the poet's son-in-law, who himself dismisses the reliability of this work in his "Author's Note": *"Toil and Triumph* is a novel, based on incidents from the poet's life, selected with an eye to their narrative importance. Most of the dialogue and a few of the scenes are imaginary. Also, some dates and facts have been rearranged for the sake of continuity. . . . It would be a mistake to suppose that this work is a biography," Leon Goldenthal, *Toil and Triumph* (New York: Pageant, 1960), 7. The second book is an ambitious work by Goldenthal's son (Rosenfeld's grandson), Dr. Edgar Goldenthal, and deals only briefly and selectively with Rosenfeld's life. See Edgar J. Goldenthal, *Poet of the Ghetto* (Hoboken, N.J.: Ktav, 1998). The major strength of this work lies in its reproduction of documents dealing with Rosenfeld, specifically several letters written to the poet which are not found in his YIVO archive. I am deeply indebted to Dr. Goldenthal for sharing with me his father's personal collection of Rosenfeldiana, which includes some of the poet's books and correspondence, as well as letters and personal memoirs originally belonging to Rosenfeld's brother Joseph.

2. Leo Wiener, *The History of Yiddish Literature in the Nineteenth Century* (New York: Scribner's, 1899).

3. Morris Rosenfeld, "Preface," *Songs from the Ghetto,* trans. Leo Wiener (Boston: Copeland and Day, 1898).

4. Although there are many critical studies on Rosenfeld's works, particularly in Yiddish, there are very few works that address his biography, particularly his

early years. For a recent example, see Marc Miller, "Morris Rosenfeld," *Dictionary of Literary Biography: Yiddish Writers* (Columbia, S.C.: Bruccoli, Clark, Layman, forthcoming).

5. Morris Rosenfeld, "Mayn lebns geshikhte in kurtsn," in *MRb*, 26. Unless otherwise noted, all translations are my own. Rosenfeld's marriage at eighteen to his mother's cousin illuminates an example of the historical unreliability of both *Toil and Triumph* and *Poet of the Ghetto*. In the first, Leon Goldenthal describes a dramatic scene in which Rosenfeld uncovers the bride's veil and, upon discovering her great ugliness, flees the room before the completion of the ceremony. See L. Goldenthal, 31. In the second, Edgar Rosenthal picks up on this invented anecdote and further embellishes it, stating that, after Rosenfeld "took one look at the 'homeliest woman in all of Poland,' he dashed out of the synagogue and didn't stop running until he reached Amsterdam!" E. J. Goldenthal, 3.

6. See *MRb*, 29.

7. On the history of the beginnings of the Yiddish press in the United States, see Moyshe Shtarkman, "Di anshteyung fun der yidishe prese in amerike," in *Zamlbukh tsu der geshikhte fun der yidishe prese in amerike*, ed. Yankev Shatsky (New York: Yidisher kultur gezelshaft, 1934), 13–21.

8. *Di post* was a weekly newspaper published intermittently in New York for six months (August 1870-January 1871). See ibid.

9. Sh. Niger's characterization serves as title to one of his numerous articles on the origins of Yiddish literature in America: "Mer altheymish vi amerikanish," *Di tsukunft*, Apr. 1940, 212–17.

10. "Di programe," *Di nyu yorker yidishe folkstsaytung*, June 25, 1886, 1.

11. For a standard work that treats the Hibbat Zion (Love of Zion) movement within the larger Zionist context, see David Vital, *The Origins of Zionism* (Oxford: Clarendon Press, 1975), 135–86. For an excellent collection of primary sources and documents that deal with this subject, see Alter Druyanow, *Ketavim Le-toldot hibbat zion ve-yishuv erets-yisrael* (Tel-Aviv: Hakibutz hameuhad, 1982).

12. For a comprehensive history of *Di nyu yorker yidishe folkstsaytung*, see Yekhezkel Lifshitz, "Di nyu yorker yidishe folkstsaytung," in *Pinkes far der forshung fun der yidisher literatur un prese*, ed. Khayim Bez (New York: Congress for Jewish Culture, 1975), 3:251–318.

13. One excellent example is H. N. Bialik's first Yiddish poem, "Nokh a yorhundert" (One More Century), which offers an ambitious, poetic perspective on the entire nineteenth century. See H. N. Bialik, "Nokh a yorhundert," *Der yid* 16 (1899). Bialik prevented the republication of this poem during his lifetime. An earlier instance of this genre is one of Morris Vinchevsky's first Yiddish works entitled

"Rikblik af dem yor T[a]RM[a]D" (Looking Back on the Year 1884). Morris Vinchevsky, *Lider un gedikhte* (New York: Frayheyt, 1910), 257. See also Elyokim Zunser, "Der nayntsntn yorhundert," in *Tsvantsik yidishe folks lider* (New York: n.p., 1898), 74–80, and Dovid Edelshtat, "Tsum yor 1891," in *Edelshtats shriftn* (New York: Hebrew, 1923), 155–56.

14. Yehuda Leyb Gordon, *Kitvei Yehuda Leyb Gordon: Shirah* (Tel-Aviv: Dvir, 1956), 17. The translation cited here is from Michael Stanislawski, *For Whom Do I Toil: Jeudah Leib Gordon and the Crisis of Russian Jewry* (New York: Oxford Univ. Press, 1988), 49.

15. Mikhl Gordon, "Shtey uf mayn folk," in *Shirei M. Gordon: Yidishe lider fun Mikhl Gordon* (Warsaw: n.p., 1889), 29–35. In a footnote, Gordon remarks that his poem was first published in 1869.

16. Morris Rosenfeld, "Dos yor 1886," *Di nyu yorker yidishe folkstsaytung*, Dec. 17, 1886, 5.

17. Morris Rosenfeld, *Di gloke: Folks lider und revolutsiyonere gedikhte* (New York: Gordon, 1888).

18. Schiller's "Das Lied von der Glocke" was especially influential among nineteenth-century Hebrew and Yiddish poets.

19. Yankev M. Merison, "Tsu 'Moris Rozenfelds onheyb,'" in *Pinkes* (New York: YIVO, 1927–28), 269. Merison wrote this essay in response to Moyshe Shtarkman's article in the same volume, "Moris Rozenfelds onheyb," 53–57.

20. Morris Rosenfeld, "Vorrede," in *Lieder des Ghetto,* trans. Berthold Feiwel (Berlin: H. Seemann Nachfolge, 1902), 4. Rosenfeld's *Di gloke* may have been the first book of Yiddish poetry ever published in the United States. The first book published in America containing Yiddish poetry is Yakov Tsvi Sobel's bilingual He-brew-Yiddish collection of poems entitled *Shir zahav likhvod yisrael hazaken/Yisrol der alte* (New York: n.p., 1877). On the beginnings of the Yiddish press and book trade in the United States, see Kalman Marmor, "Der onheyb fun a yidisher liter-atur in amerike," in *Almanakh fun internatsiyonaln arbeter ordn* (New York: Jewish National Workers' Alliance, 1940), 335–64.

21. See Rosenfeld, *Di gloke.* "Tsu mayn folk" (37–40), is a slightly reworked version of "Dos yor 1886," and "Di muter an dos kind" (42–45) first appeared as "Dos vign-lid" in *Di nyu yorker yidishe folkstsaytung,* Jan. 14, 1887, 6.

22. The following poems in Rosenfeld's *Di gloke* were first published in *Arbeter fraynd* with few changes: "Der veker der frayheyt" (53), first published June 1, 1888; "Di revolutsiyon" (61), first published July 6, 1888; "Vi lang nokh?" (34–35), "Biz danen!" (35–36) and "Un alzo" (36–37), first published September 14, 1888.

23. Rosenfeld, *Di gloke,* 6.

24. Ibid., 9.

25. On the Lucian tradition in the Hebrew literature of the *haskala*, see Shmuel Werses, "Hedei hasatira shel lukianus be-sifrut ha-haskala ha-ivrit," in *Megamot ve-tsurot be sifrut ha-haskalah* (Jerusalem: Magnes Press, 1990), 223–48.

26. Two notable early contributions by Rosenfeld to *Di tsukunft* include the first versions of his well-known poems "Mayn yingele" and "In shap," the latter of which he later titled "Di svet shap," *Di tsukunft*, Jan. 1893, 9.

27. Zalman Reyzn, *Leksikon fun der yidisher literatur, prese, un philologiye* (Vilna: Vilner farlag, 1916), 667–68.

28. From July 18, 1890, to January 13, 1893, Rosenfeld published twenty-six poems in the *Arbeter tsaytung*.

29. Morris Rosenfeld, *Di blumenkete: A zamlung fun farshidene folks lider un poeziyen* (New York, Folksadvokat, 1890).

30. "Nachtgedanken" was originally published in Heine's collection *Neue Gedichte*. See Heinrich Heine, *Sämtliche Werke* (Leipzig: Tempel, 1910), 1:352–54. Edward Young wrote his "Night Thoughts" in 1742–45, and it was one of the most influential poems of the eighteenth century. Unlike much of the poetry produced during this era, Young's work is a decidedly non-neoclassical poem. This sentimental work was very popular, particularly in Germany, where it influenced writers of the Sturm und Drang movement such as Friedrich Gottlieb Klopstock (1724–1803).

31. The motif of death as an approaching ship originated in the Charon tradition of Greek mythology.

32. Morris Rosenfeld, "Nakht gedankn," in *Di blumenkete*, 3.

33. Morris Rosenfeld, *Poeziyen un lider. Ershter teyl: Natsionele lider* (New York: A. H. Rosenberg, 1893).

34. Ibid., 19.

35. Ibid., 21–22.

36. Morris Rosenfeld, *Lider bukh: Ershter teyl* (New York: Grover Brothers, 1897).

37. Morris Rosenfeld, "Tsu mayne verte abonentn," in ibid., 1.

38. The dedication to Rosenfeld's *Lider bukh* reads: "This work is dedicated with honor and respect to my worthy friend Leo Wiener, professor of Slavic languages at Harvard College."

39. In Rosenfeld's first collected works, *Gezamlte lider* (New York: A. M. Evalenko, 1904), and in all subsequent editions of Rosenfeld's works, this poem is entitled "Di svet shap."

40. Wiener, iv–ix.

41. On the mutually beneficial exchange between Rosenfeld and Wiener, see Yekhezkel Lifshitz, "Moris Rozenfeld un Leo Viner," *Fraye arbeter shtime,* July 15, 1962, 5. See also Sarah Alisa Braun, "Translating the Ghetto: Leo Wiener, Morris Rosenfeld and the Invention of a Yiddish Poet," in "Becoming Authorities: Jews, Writing and the Dynamics of Literary Affiliation, 1890–1940," Ph.D. diss., University of Michigan, in progress, and Susan Klingenstein, "A Philologist: The Adventures of Leo Wiener (1862–1939)," in *Jews in the American Academy, 1900–1940: The Dynamics of Intellectual Assimilation* (Syracuse: Syracuse Univ. Press, 1998), 8–17.

42. Rosenfeld to Leo Wiener, Mar. 29, 1898, in *MRb,* 68–69.

43. See *MRb,* 70.

44. See *MRb, 73.* The Lower East Side College Settlement was opened in 1889 and was located at 95 Rivington Street on New York's Lower East Side. Run by women, this organization served as a type of neighborhood house that housed a library, kindergarten, as well as offered classes and lectures. The success of the College Settlement spawned sister institutions in the 1890s in Baltimore, Boston and Philadelphia. See Jane Allen, "College Settlement," in *Encyclopedia of New York City,* ed. Kenneth T. Jackson (New Haven: Yale Univ. Press, 1995), 254.

45. Morris Rosenfeld, *Songs from the Ghetto,* trans. Leo Wiener, 2nd ed. (Boston: Small, Maynard and Company, 1900).

46. Dean Howells's review of *Songs from the Ghetto* appeared in *Literature,* Feb. 10, 1899. In *The Nation,* Sept. 9, 1897, Leo Wiener wrote a very favorable review of Rosenfeld's recently published *Lider bukh.* Many articles appeared in the American literary press on Rosenfeld before the publication of *Songs from the Ghetto.* These pieces praised the author and announced the upcoming publication of his book in publications such as *The Transcript* (Boston), Feb. 18, 1898; *The Bookman,* Mar. 1898; *The New York Journal,* Mar. 27, 1898; *The Public Ledger* (Philadelphia), Apr. 25, 1898; and an advertisement for *Songs from the Ghetto* in the *Atlantic Monthly,* Oct. 1898. Positive reviews of the book were written in prominent literary publications such as *The Dial,* Jan. 16, 1899; *The Book Buyer,* Feb. 1899; *The Saturday Evening Post,* Feb. 4, 1899; *The Bookman,* Apr. 1899; and *The Critic,* Mar. 1900.

47. On Rosenfeld and his experience writing English poetry, see Ezekiel Lifshutz, "Morris Rosenfeld Attempts to Become an English Poet," *American Jewish Archives* 2, no. 22 (Nov. 1970): 121–37. Lifshutz includes several of Rosenfeld's English-language poems among the hundreds in the YIVO archive. See also A. Leyeles, "M. Rozenfeld: 'Englisher poet,' " *Tog-Morgn Zhurnal,* June 10, 1962, 14.

48. Mordkhe Dantses, "A fertl yorhundert bagegenishn mit Moris Rozenfeld," *Der tog,* July 15, 1933, 5. Morris Rosenfeld, "I Know Not Why," in *An American Anthology, 1787–1899,* ed. Edmund Clarence Stedman (Boston: Houghton, Mifflin,

1900). This poem is also reprinted in Hutchins Hapgood's 1902 *Spirit of the Ghetto* (Cambridge, Mass.: Belknap Press, 1967).

49. Rabbi Stephen Wise to Morris Rosenfeld, Feb. 6, 1899. This letter belongs to Dr. Edgar Goldenthal and is reprinted in E. J. Goldenthal, 362.

50. See *MRb*, 80–81, 82.

51. Mort Shlossman, "Memories of Morris Rosenfeld," *Jewish News* (Newark, N.J.), June 29, 1962, 20.

52. See *MRb*, 85.

53. Rosenfeld to Leo Wiener, Feb. 14, 1899, in *MRb*, 86. This letter is reprinted in *Poet of the Ghetto*, 361.

54. Rosenfeld to Leo Wiener, May 14, 1899, in *MRb*, 95.

55. Rosenfeld to Leo Wiener, July 14, 1899, in *MRb*, 100.

56. See *MRb*, 78.

57. See *MRb*, 83–88.

58. See *MRb*, 100–101.

59. *Der pinkes* 1 (April, 1900). Reprinted in *MRb*, 103.

60. On the history of *Di yidishe velt*, see Yitskhok Fayn, "Di yidishe velt (Louis Marshalls batsiyung tsu yidish)," in *Pinkes far der forshung fun der yidisher literatur un prese* (New York: Congress for Jewish Culture, 1975), 3:334–44.

61. On his loyalty to the socialist cause, see Rosenfeld's letter to Reuven Braynin from the end of 1914 in which he states: "Although not a member of the So-cialist Party, I always vote for the Socialist ticket," *MRb*, 157.

62. Translations of Rosenfeld's collected poems, almost all based on Wiener's English-language renditions in *Songs from the Ghetto*, appeared in the following lan-guages: Polish: *Wiazanka*, trans. Israel Waldman (Stanislav: Nakladem ksiegar E. Weidenfelda I Brata, 1903) and *Piesni Pracy*, trans. Samuel Hirszhorn and Alfred Tom (Warsaw: n.p., 1906); Romanian: *Cintece din Ghetto*, trans. M. Rusu (Jasi: Ili-escu, Grossu, 1904); Czech: *Zpevy z Ghetta*, trans. Yaroslav Verkhlitski (Prague: n.p., 1903); Serbian: *Pjesme iz geta*, trans. Alexander Likht (Zagreb: n.p., 1906); Hungar-ian: *Költeményei*, trans. Arnold Kiss (Budapest: Deutsch Z. és Társa könyvk-ereskedese, 1908); German: *Gedichte von Morris Rosenfeld*, trans. Friedrich Thiberger, intro. Friedrich Adler. (Prague: Richard Brandeis, 1909).

63. On Moses Lilien's illustrations for *Lieder des Ghetto*, see Michael Stanis-lawski, "Vom Jugendstil zum 'Judenstil': Universalismus und Nationalismus im Werk Ephraim Moses Liliens," in *Zionistische Utopie: Israelische Realität*, ed. Michael Brenner and Yfaat Weiss (Munich: C. H. Beck, 1999), 87–95.

64. See *MRb*, 37.

65. Rosenfeld to Dov-Ber Terkel, Dec. 7, 1904, in *MRb*, 112.

66. See Rosenfeld to Shaul Ginsburg, Feb. 4, 1905, in *MRb*, 108–9, written three months before his son died.

67. See Rosenfeld to Kalman Marmor, Mar. 1, 1906, in *MRb*, 122.

68. Joseph Rosenfeld to Leo Wiener, May 25, 1906, in *MRb*, 118. See also Rosenfeld to Leo Wiener, Feb. 13, 1898, in *MRb*, 59: "You are my savior . . . I have you to thank for much, if not everything."

69. See *MRb*, 104.

70. Yekhezkel Lifshitz cites a letter dated November 6, 1906, which Professor Seligman wrote to Rosenfeld's wife. In it, Seligman tells her that he instructed his brother to send her a monthly check for five dollars. See *MRb*, 123.

71. See *MRb*, 123. In his *Leksikon fun der yidisher literatur* (Vilna: Vilner farlag, 1928), 155, Zalman Reyzn writes that Sholem Aleykhem published an appeal for help on behalf of the sick poet. Although I have been unable to locate the source of this citation, Sholem Aleykhem makes reference to it in a letter to Y. Kh. Ravnitski and Kh. N. [H. N.] Bialik. Dated "New York, December 12, 1906," Sholem Aleykhem refers to the "appeal" which he made the previous day in support of the bedridden Rosenfeld. See Y. D. Berkovich, ed., *Dos Sholem Aleykhem bukh*, 2nd ed. (New York: YKUF, 1958), 215.

72. See *MRb*, 124–27. See also Rabbi A. B. Rhine to *American Israelite* (Cincinnati), Sept. 25, 1906, in *MRb*, 107, in which Rabbi Rhine appeals to the editor to champion the cause of the sick and impoverished poet and to raise money on his behalf.

73. Rosenfeld to Kalman Marmor, Mar. 15, 1907, in *MRb*, 128.

74. Rosenfeld to Vilna *Folkstsaytung*, Feb. 18, 1907, in *MRb*, 127.

75. In Yiddish, the adjective *piskate* means "noisy or foulmouthed." In *A Little Love in Big Manhattan* (Cambridge, Mass.: Harvard Univ. Press, 1988), Ruth Wisse translates this moniker as "Berl the Piece Cutter," implying a "Yinglish" title for the character.

76. Morris Rosenfeld, *Shriftn fun Moris Rozenfeld* (New York: A. M. Yevalenko, 1908–10).

77. See Berkovich, 366.

78. Rosenfeld's travel installments were published in the *Forverts* in the latter months of 1908 and collected in volume six of Rosenfeld, *Shriftn*. Collectively, Rosenfeld entitled these installments *Rayze bilder*, a reference to the famous work by Heine of the same name. Indeed, Rosenfeld makes numerous references to the German poet in these pieces. See also "Moris Rozenfelds rayze iber estraykh un daytshland," *Forverts*, Dec. 26, 1908, 4.

79. For two treatments of Di yunge, see Ruth R. Wisse, "Di Yunge and the

Problem of Jewish aestheticism," *Jewish Social Studies* 38 (Summer-Fall 1976): 265–76 and "Di Yunge: Immigrants or Exiles?" *Prooftexts* 1, no. 1 (Jan. 1981): 43–61. For a more comprehensive treatment of two specific poets of this generation, Moyshe-Leyb Halpern and Mani Leyb, see Wisse, *Little Love.*

80. See, for example, the article by Moyshe-Leyb Halpern, "An ofener briv tsu Moris Rozenfeld," *Der kibitzer,* Dec. 2, 1910.

81. *Der baytsh,* Nov. 12, 1908, 1.

82. Morris Rosenfeld, *Geveylte shriftn* (New York: Forward, 1912).

83. See "2,000 Cheer for Poet Rosenfeld and His Verses," *Chicago Examiner,* Dec. 29, 1913.

84. See *MRb,* 163–68.

85. Rosenfeld to Reuven Braynin, 1914, in *MRb,* 157. Although Rosenfeld dates this letter dated only "1914," Lifshitz dates it in the late months of 1914.

86. Morris Rosenfeld, *Dos bukh fun libe* (New York: M. Gurevitch, 1914).

87. Morris Rosenfeld, "Dem dikhters forvert," in ibid., 6. See also Rosenfeld to Yekhezkel Levit, Sept. 13, 1914, in *MRb,* 169–70.

88. Rosenfeld to Yekhezkel Levit, Sept. 27, 1914, in *MRb,* 174–75.

89. See Kalman Marmor, "Moris Rozenfelds satirishe lider kegn der geler prese in amerike," *Visnshaft un revolutsiye* (Jan.-March 1935): 3–9. Following his article, Marmor published his own edited version of Rosenfeld's *Di shraybarniye,* which the poet assembled for publication, most probably as a section of the book that he planned to publish, entitled *Kas un shmeykhl* (Anger and Smile). Rosenfeld had assembled the poems which appeared in the Yiddish press, mostly in *Yidishe shtime,* alongside his own manuscripts.

90. In American Yiddish, *soker* (sucker) does not have the same meaning that *sucker* does in current English usage. Here it connotes "swindler" or "crook."

91. Morris Rosenfeld, *Grine tsores un andere shriftn* (New York: Literatur, 1919).

92. The "Songs of a Pilgrim" project was so close to being realized that the Jewish Forum published an advertisement in 1919 stating that "Morris Rosenfeld, the Leading Yiddish Poet Has Written a Volume of English Poems entitled 'Songs of a Pilgrim.' Subscribers to the magazine could renew their annual subscriptions for $2.50 and receive a free copy of this new book, or they could purchase the book alone for $1.50. In Rosenfeld's archive at YIVO, there are several copies of this manuscript, which contains approximately one hundred poems.

93. Kalman Marmor printed a photocopy of the *Tageblat*'s termination letter to Rosenfeld, dated March 4, 1921, in "Fun Moris Rozenfelds literarishe yerushe," *Pinkes* (New York: YIVO, 1927–28), 1, 210.

94. This mailing from the Y. L. Perets shrayber farayn can be found in Morris Rosenfeld's YIVO archive.

95. See, for example, Rosenfeld's obituary in the *New York Times*, Friday, June 22, 1923.

96. An especially prolific year was 1962, the anniversary of Rosenfeld's one hundredth birthday, when scores of articles and a volume of selected poetry and articles edited by the literary critic Nakhman Mayzl and entitled *Tsum hundertstn geburtstog fun Moris Rozenfeld* (New York: YIKUF, 1962) were published in the Yiddish press.

97. Abraham Cahan, "Moris Rozenfeld," *Forverts*, June 23, 1923, 3.

98. *Forverts*, June 25, 1923, 1.

2. The Appropriation of Morris Rosenfeld

1. Louis Budianov, "A blondzhender poet," *Der nayer gayst* 1, no. 2 (Nov. 1897): 103–07.

2. Ibid., 106.

3. Leon Kobrin, "A blondzhender kritik (an entfer af Herr Budianovs artikl 'a blondzhender poet')," *Der nayer gayst* 1, no. 3 (Dec. 1897): 168–72.

4. It seems that the editorial board at *Der nayer gayst* (under the control of Alexander Harkavy) did not fully agree with Kobrin's assertion that Jews are not a nation: they placed a question mark in parentheses after it. Ibid., 171.

5. Yankev Milkh, " 'Printsipiyele kritik': An antvort af L. Kobrins 'blondzhende kritik,' " *Der nayer gayst* 1, no. 4 (Jan. 1898): 242–46; no. 5 (Feb. 1898): 292–97.

6. Ibid., no. 5 (Feb. 1898): 293.

7. See Dan Miron, "A Language as Caliban," in *A Traveler Disguised* (New York: Schocken Books, 1973), 34–66.

8. I. F. Marcosson, "A Voice from the Ghetto," *Bookman* 9, no. 1 (Mar. 1899): 68.

9. William Morton Payne, "Rosenfeld's *Songs from the Ghetto*," *Dial*, Jan. 16, 1899, 54.

10. Consider the titles of the following articles about Rosenfeld at this time which stress his supposed authenticity: "Real Poet Found in New York's East Side," *New York Journal*, Mar. 27, 1898; "Two Poets of New York's Ghetto," *New York Herald*, July 5, 1903; "A Ghetto Poet," *Public Ledger* (Philadelphia), Apr. 25, 1898.

11. See note 62 for chapter 1.

12. Berthold Feiwel, in Rosenfeld, *Lieder des Ghetto*, 16.

13. Meyer Isser Pinès, "Histoire de la littérature judéo-allemande," Ph.D. diss., Univ. of Paris, 1910.

14. Meyer Isser Pinès, *Di geshikhte fun der yidisher literatur*, ed. Bal Makhshoves (Warsaw: B. Shimin, 1911). This work was subsequently published in German. See

Meyer Isser Pinès, *Die Geschichte der jüdischdeutschen Literatur,* trans. Georg Hecht (Leipzig: G. Engel, 1913).

15. Sh. Niger, "Moris Rozenfeld (tsu zayn 50-yorikn yubiley)," *Di yidishe velt* 5 (May 1913): 93.

16. Ibid., 96.

17. Borukh Rivkin, *Grunt tendensn fun der yidisher literatur in amerike* (New York: YKUF, 1948), 61–77. The section on Rosenfeld is a slightly reworked version of his earlier essay "Moris Rozenfeld: Der ershter oystsubafrayen zayn lid fun unter der takhlis-distsiplin," in *Yidishe dikhter in amerike* (New York: CYCO, 1947), 1:35–48.

18. Avrom Tabachnik, *Dikhter un dikhtung* (New York: Knight, 1965), 5.

19. Ibid.

20. Ibid., 4–5.

21. Ibid, 12.

22. Nakhman Mayzl, "Moris Rozenfeld," in *Noente un vayte* (Vilna: B. Kletskin, 1926), 32–40.

23. Ibid, 33.

24. Ibid., 39.

25. Sol Liptzin, *The Flowering of Yiddish Literature* (New York: Thomas Yoseloff, 1963), 140, 143.

26. Charles Madison, *Yiddish Literature: Its Scope and Major Writers* (New York: Frederick Ungar, 1968), 157.

27. Ibid., 163.

28. For a study of this period, see David A. Hollinger, *In the American Province: Studies in the History and Historiography of Ideas* (Baltimore: Johns Hopkins Univ. Press, 1985).

29. Morris Rosenfeld, "Berl der piskater vert a dekadent," *Forverts,* Nov. 20, 1910. See note 75 for chapter 1.

30. Halpern, "An ofener briv," 10, 15.

31. On humoristic and satiric Yiddish publications, see Khone Gotesfeld, "Di humoristishe zhurnaln: Der 'Kibitser' un 'Groyser kundes,' " *75 yor yidishe prese in amerike,* ed. Y. Glatshteyn, Sh. Niger, and H. Rogof (New York: Yiddish Writers Union, 1945), 97–99. See also Edward Portnoy, "The Creation of a Jewish Cartoon Space in the Yiddish Presses of New York and Warsaw, 1889–1939," Ph.D. diss., Jewish Theological Seminary of America, 2006.

32. Although a subsequent anthology did not live up to the ambitious publication program of the first, Halpern did edit, along with Menakhem, another anthology the following year that was intended as a continuation of *Fun mentsh tsu mentsh* entitled *Ist brodvey.*

33. Reuven Ayzland, "Di naye vendung in der yidisher poeziye," in *Fun mentsh tsu mentsh*, ed. M.-L. Halpern (New York: Farlag nyu york, 1915), 32–36.

34. See, for example, Dovid Ignatov "Di yugnt," *Di yugnt* 2 (Jan. 1908): 1–2; Yoyl Entin, "A yidisher romantizm," in *Troymn un virklekhkeyt*, ed. Y. Adler and Y. Slonim (New York: n.p., 1909): 14–24; R. Ayzland, "Di yunge," *Shriftn* 1 (1912): 3–20; Dovid Ignatov, "Sheyne grobyungeray un mise grobyungeray," *Shriftn* 1 (1912): 3–11. Each article in *Shriftn* has its own separate pagination.

35. Zisho Lande, introduction, in *Di yidishe dikhtung in amerike biz yor 1919*, ed. Zisho Lande (New York: Farlag yidish, 1919), iv.

36. Ibid., vii.

37. Rosenfeld, *Shriftn* 1:177.

38. Morris Rosenfeld, "Yeshaye," in Lande, 148. This poem, in its original form, is an adaptation of chapter 35 in Isaiah. In his editing of this text, Lande bases his emendation on the original text, specifically the beginning of verse seven: "The burning sand shall become a pool, and the thirsty ground springs of water."

39. Morris Rosenfeld, "In zayn hand," in Lande, 149.

40. Moyshe-Leyb Halpern, "Der alter un der nayer Moris Rozenfeld," *Literatur un lebn* (Mar. 1915): 100–112.

41. Ibid., 106.

42. Ibid.

43. For a detailed discussion of the persona "Moyshe-Leyb," see Marc Miller, "Modernism and Persona in the Works of Moyshe-Leyb Halpern," *Yiddish* 11, no. 1 (1998): 48–71.

44. Halpern, "Der alter," 105.

45. Nokhem Borekh Minkov, "Moris Rozenfeld," in *Yidishe klasiker-poetn* (New York: Bidermanis farlag, 1937), 67–98.

46. Nokhem Borekh Minkov, *Pionern fun yidisher poeziye in amerike* (New York: Grenich, 1956), 1:14.

47. Yankev Glatshteyn, "Moris Rozenfelds briv" (1956), in *In tokh genumen* (Buenos Aires: YIVO, 1960), 1:152. This is a collection of Glatshteyn's essays culled from the Yiddish press and dated individually.

48. Yankev Glatshteyn, "Moris Rozenfeld," in *Mit mayne fartogbikher* (Tel-Aviv: Farlag Y. L. Peretz, 1963), 329–66.

49. Ibid., 361.

50. Ibid., 337, 338, 339.

51. Rosenfeld, *Shriftn*, 2:59. Other, very personal poems in which Rosenfeld addresses the death of his son can be found in this same volume and include "Mayn zun," "Mayn kind," "Ale shvaygn," and "Erd," 54–58.

52. For a schematic survey of the critical reception of American Sweatshop po-

etry in Soviet Yiddish criticism, with a particular focus on the critique and publication of the works of Dovid Edelshtat, see Alexander Pomerants, "Politishe kritik," in *Di sovetishe harugey malokhes* (Buenos Aires: YIVO, 1962), 302–30. See also Marc Miller, "Tradition and Hegemony: Soviet Yiddish Literary Critics and American Sweatshop Poetry in the Interwar Period," *East European Jewish Affairs* 35, no. 2 (Dec. 2005): 189–207.

53. *Di varheyt* was founded in March 1918 in Petrograd as the "Organ of the S.D. Bolsheviks and Left Socialist-Revolutionaries." The publication moved its headquarters to Moscow in May 1918; in August of the same year, it changed its title to *Der emes*. This newly renamed publication was the first daily Yiddish Communist newspaper in postrevolutionary Russia. It maintained its original Hebrew spelling until its demise in February 1919. On November 7, 1920, a new daily, which essentially would serve as the Yiddish counterpart to the Russian *Pravda*, was established in Moscow. Although also called *Der emes*, in a break with tradition, the new publication spelled its title phonetically. For a survey and analysis of Soviet Yiddish orthography, particularly in relation to the Hebrew element of Yiddish, see Rakhmiel Peltz, "The Dehebraization Controversy in Soviet Yiddish Language Planning: Standard or Symbol?" in *Readings in the Sociology of Jewish Languages*, ed. Joshua Fishman (Leiden: E. J. Brill, 1985), 125–50. For bibliographic information on Soviet Yiddish publications in the interwar period, see Khone Shmeruk, *Pirsumim yehudiim bevrit hamoatsot, 1917–60* (Jerusalem: Historical Society of Israel, 1961).

54. Yoysef Bovshover, *Geklibene lider* (Petrograd: Tsentraler yidisher komisariyat, 1918).

55. Moyshe Litvakov, "Yerushe un hegemoniye," *Der emes*, Feb. 14, 1926. This article was reprinted in the second volume of Litvakov's collection of essays *In umru* (Moscow: Shul un bukh, 1926), 5–28, from which I have quoted.

56. Litvakov, *In umru*, 7.

57. Ibid., 9.

58. Ibid.

59. Avrom Vevyorke, "Arop mitn kleynbirglekhn kheyrem," *Der emes*, Apr. 10, 1927. This article is reprinted in Vevyorke's book *In shturem* (Kharkov: Melukhisher Natsmindfarlag, 1932), 41–46, from which I have quoted.

60. Vevyorke, *In shturem*, 43. *Badkhones* is a type of poetry that originated with the oral rhymes of popular entertainers. Such poems were often traditional style ballads set to music and performed at weddings. Eventually, traveling musicians visited different towns and cities in the Jewish Pale of Settlement in the Russian empire and performed these compositions for crowds. The more famous published performers include Elyokim Zunser and Mikhl Gordon. Perceived by many

literary critics as premodern, *badkhones* often carries pejorative, subliterary connotations.

61. Ibid., 44.

62. Ibid.

63. Ibid., 46.

64. Avrom Vevyorke, *Reviziye* (Kharkov: Melukhe-Farlag Literatur un Kunst, 1931).

65. Avrom Vevyorke, "Reviziye," *Prolit* 2 (May 1928): 27–36; quotation is from Pomerants, 309–10.

66. Meyer Viner, "Tsu der problem fun literarisher yerushe" (dated "Kiev, Nov. 1931") in *Problemes fun kritik,* ed. M. Viner and A. Gurshteyn, eds. (Moscow: Emes, 1933), 131–75, from which I have quoted. An abbreviated version, dated April 26, 1932, was published in the Minsk literary journal *Shtern* 4–5 (Apr.-May 1932): 120–43.

67. Meyer Viner, in Viner and Gurshteyn, 132.

68. Vevyorke's "Undzer yikhes" (Our Pedigree) first appeared in three install-ments in *Shtern* 4 (Apr. 1930): 80–90; 5–6 (May-June 1930): 132–39; and 7–8 (July-Aug. 1930): 76–80. These three articles were collected and elaborated on the following year and published as a chapter in Vevyorke's book *Reviziye* as "Undzer yikhes," 97–168. I have quoted from this later, expanded text.

69. Dovid Kurland, ed., *Di ershte yidishe arbeter-dikhter (Moris Vinchevsky, Moris Rozenfeld, Dovid Edelshtat, Yoysef Bovshover)* (Moscow: Tsentraler Felker-Farlag fun F.S.S.R., Belorussian Section, 1931).

70. Ibid., 18.

71. Moyshe Litvakov, "Vegn di ershte proletarishe dikhter," in *Af tsvey frontn* (Moscow: Tsentraler Felker-Farlag fun F.S.S.R., 1931), 173.

72. Nicholas Timasheff, *The Great Retreat: The Growth and Decline of Communism in Russia* (New York: Dutton, 1946).

73. "Der zeyde" (the Grandfather) calls to mind the epithet given to S. Y. Abramovitch's authorial persona Mendele Moykher Sforim by Sholem Aleykhem, and which occupies a dominant position in Yiddish literary criticism.

74. See M. Levitan, "Vegn Edelshtat's publitsistik," *Visnshaft un revolutsiye* 3–4 (July-Dec. 1934): 147–59.

75. Moyshe Basin, ed., *Amerikaner yidishe poeziye antologiye* (New York: n.p., 1940).

76. Ibid., 6.

77. Although the *American Yiddish Poetry Anthology* does not aim to be a com-pletely historical compilation of Yiddish poetry in America, its selections have been made both on aesthetic grounds and on the perceived historical worth of the indi-

vidual poets, particularly those who preceded Di yunge. Thus, whereas poets such as Morris Rosenfeld, Avrom Reyzn, and A. Liyesen are represented, Rosenfeld's most famous contemporaries, Yoysev Bovshover, Dovid Edelshtat, and Morris Vinchevsky, are not, let alone his lesser-known ones.

78. Irving Howe and Eliezer Greenberg, eds., *A Treasury of Yiddish Poetry* (New York: Holt, Rinehart and Winston, 1969). Howe also coedited the prose counterpart to this volume, Irving Howe and Eliezer Greenberg, eds., *A Treasury of Yiddish Stories* (New York: Viking, 1954). Both are self-declared projects to rescue Yiddish culture from annihilation. As such, they are dedicated to the victims of the mid-twentieth-century European destruction of the Jews, the former "To the Yiddish Writers Destroyed by Hitler and Stalin," and the latter "To the Six Million."

Irving Howe began his career as a scholar of English-language literature, writing books on American authors such as Edith Wharton and Sherwood Anderson. In the 1970s, he dedicated himself to researching East European Jews, and, in particular, to Yiddish. In this decade, he wrote his best-selling treatment of the Jewish immigration to and settlement of the Lower East Side in *World of Our Fathers*, with Kenneth Libo (New York: Simon and Schuster, 1976), as well as *How We Lived: A Documentary History of Immigrant Jews in America, 1880–1930*, with Kenneth Libo (New York: R. Marek, 1979). Howe and Eliezer Greenberg coedited several anthologies of Yiddish literature including *Voices from the Yiddish: Essays, Memoirs, Diaries* (Ann Arbor: Univ. of Michigan Press, 1972); *Yiddish Stories, Old and New* (New York: Holiday House, 1974); and *Ashes Out of Hope: Fiction by Soviet-Yiddish Writers* (New York: Schocken Books, 1977).

79. Irving Howe, Ruth R. Wisse, and Khone Shmeruk, eds., *The Penguin Book of Modern Yiddish Verse* (New York: Viking, 1987).

80. Indeed, the one older writer whose poetry is well represented in both *The Penguin Book of Modern Yiddish Verse* and *A Treasury of Yiddish Poetry* is Avrom Reyzn, whom Howe greatly appreciated.

81. Ruth R. Wisse, *What Shall Live and What Shall Die: The Makings of a Yiddish Anthology.* (Cincinnati: Univ. of Cincinnati, Judaic Studies Program, 1989), 12.

82. Benjamin and Barbara Harshav, eds., *American Yiddish Poetry* (Berkeley: Univ. of California Press, 1986).

3. The Melodramatic and Sentimental Sweatshop

1. There are numerous examples of ideologically freighted exhortative poetry in the works of Rosenfeld's contemporaries. Some of the best known are Dovid Edelshtat's "Tsu mayn feder" and "Tsum arbeter," in Edelshtat, 6–8, 199; Yoysef Bovshover's "Tsu mayn muze" and "Tsum vind," in *Gezamlte shriftn* (New York:

Fraye arbeter shtime, 1911), 7–9, 14; Morris Vinchevsky's "Tsum arbeter," in *Gezamlte verk* (New York, 1927), 18–19.

2. M. H. Abrams, *Natural Supernaturalism: Tradition and Revolution in Romantic Literature* (New York: Norton, 1971), 63.

3. Ibid., 62–63.

4. Ibid.

5. Ibid., 63.

6. Before immigrating to America, while working in London sweatshops between 1883 and 1886, Rosenfeld wrote the first poems that he set to music, intending them to be sung by his fellow shop workers. Thus, in "Der shnayder verkshap," the subtitle instructs readers that this poem is meant "tsum zingen," (to be sung). See Rosenfeld, *Di gloke*, 15–16.

7. Yoysef Bovshover, "A gezang tsum folk," in *Gezamlte shriftn*, 45. The last word in this stanza is pronounced "doyres" in standard Yiddish. I have rendered it as *deyres* because that represents the Lithuanian dialectical pronunciation that Bovshover employs for the sake of rhyme (*peyres-deyres*), as he does in many of his poems.

8. Dovid Edelshtat, "In kamf," in Edelshtat, 15.

9. Ibid., 16.

10. Morris Vinchevsky, "Di tsukunft," in *Gezamlte verk*, 2:87. The word *rayen* (lines) is pronounced "reyen" in standard Yiddish, but, for the poem's rhyme, it is pronounced here in the Central or Polish dialect.

11. Morris Vinchevsky, "Dray shvester," in *Gezamlte verk*, 2:42.

12. Ibid.

13. Morris Rosenfeld, "Der tsveyfakher may," in *Di blumenkete*, 36.

14. Morris Rosenfeld, "Lebnsbilder," *Di gloke*, 12–23.

15. Morris Rosenfeld, "Ambelens," in ibid., 13.

16. Robert Bechtold Heilman, *Tragedy and Melodrama: Versions of Experience* (Seattle: Univ. of Washington Press, 1968), 72–73.

17. Ibid., 79.

18. Ibid.

19. Ibid.

20. Rosenfeld, "Di svet shap," *Shriftn*, 1:8. Unless otherwise noted, all page numbers for Rosenfeld's Sweatshop poems appear in the main text and refer to volume 1 of the poet's *Shriftn* (Writings).

21. Peter Brooks, *The Melodramatic Imagination: Balzac, Henry James, Melodrama, and the Mode of Excess*, 2nd ed. (New Haven: Yale Univ. Press, 1995).

22. Joanne Dobson, "Reclaiming Sentimental Literature," *American Literature* 69, no. 2 (June 1997): 267.

23. Morris Rosenfeld, "Di muter an dos kind," in *Di gloke*, 42–45. This poem is a slightly reworked version of Rosenfeld's "Dos vign lid" (The Lullaby), which appeared in *Di nyu yorker yidishe folkstsaytung*, Jan. 14, 1887, 6.

24. Morris Rosenfeld, "Di muter an dos kind," in *Di gloke*, 45.

25. See M. H. Abrams, "Ballad," *A Glossary of Literary Terms* (Fort Worth, 1993), 11.

26. See, for example, Morris Vinchevsky, "Dray shvester," "Dos ufele in vald," and "Kleyn-Etele," in Vinchevsky, *Gezamlte verk*, 2:42, 43–44, 51, resp.

27. See Benjamin Hrushovski (Harshav), "On Free Rhythms in Modern Yiddish Poetry," *The Field of Yiddish*, ed. Uriel Weinreich (New York: Linguistic Cirle of New York, 1954), 225. On the stanza forms of Yiddish folksongs, see also Binyamin Hrushovski (Benjamin Harshav), "Habayit hatipusi b'shir am b'yidish," in *Sefer hayovel l'Dov Sadan* (N.p: n.d.), 111–28. See also Uriel Weinreich, "On the Cultural History of Yiddish Rime," in *Essays on Jewish Life and Thought,* ed. Joseph L. Blau(New York: Columbia Univ. Press, 1959), 423–42.

28. Brooks, 20.

29. Ibid., 30–31.

30. Halpern, "Der alter," 104–5.

31. Brooks, 9.

32. Ibid., 13.

33. Morris Rosenfeld, "Tsvishn di toyte," in *Di blumenkete*, 13.

34. Morris Rosenfeld, "Di royte behole," in *Geveylte shriftn*, 1:62–63.

35. Ibid., 63.

36. This Hebrew poetic model is based on a Russian one employed, most notably, by the poet Alexei Apukhtin (1841 93).

37. Yehuda Leyb Gordon, "Zidkiyahu ve-vet ha-pekudot," in Y. L. Gordon, 98–101; see also Stanislawski, *For Whom*, 142–45.

38. Shaul Tschernikhovsky, "Barukh me-magenza," in *Poemot ve-ideliyot* (Tel-Aviv: Am Oved,, 1990), 2:17–44.

4. The "Simple" Language of the Sweatshop

1. Their intention to abandon Yiddish when the time was right has led Dan Miron to characterize *haskala* writers as "self-destructive." See Dan Miron, "Folklore and Antifolklore in the Yiddish Fiction of the Haskala," in *The Image of the Shtetl and Other Studies of Modern Jewish Literary Imagination* (Syracuse: Syracuse Univ. Press, 2000), 49–80.

2. H. N. Bialik used litotes in his poetry, most notably, in the first lines of his

epic poem "Metei midbar" (The Dead of the Desert), in *Shirim*, ed. Dan Miron (Tel-Aviv: Dvir, 2000), 3:340: "Lo adat kfirim ulvaim y'khasu sham eyn ha'arava, / Lo khvod habashan umivkhar alonav sham naflu b'adir— / Al yad ohaleykhem hakodrim mutalim bakhama anakim, / ben kholot hamidbar hatsehubim ka'arayot lavetakh yirbatsu" [A pride of lions does not cover there the eye of the plain, / Not the honor of Bashan and not the chosen of it oaks there mightily fell— / By their somber tents giants are cast down in the sun, / amid the yellow desert sand like lions in secure repose].

3. Peter Brooks, *The Melodramatic Imagination*, 15.

4. Absent a felicitous English equivalent for *daytshmerish* when used as a noun, I shall leave it in the original Yiddish.

5. New High German (NHG), which dates from 1650, is the literary language that developed out of Martin Luther's translation of the Bible (written in East Central German, 1522–34).

6. Max Weinreich, "Daytshmerish toyg nit," *Yidish far ale* 4 (June 1938): 105.

7. Mordkhe Shekhter, "Fun dizn-dazn tsun a yidish yidish," in *Laytish mameloshn* (New York: Yidish-lige, 1986), 1:56.

8. Hirshe-Dovid Kats, "A shtekele arayn, a shtekele aroys, di daytshmerishe gefar iz—oys," *Yidishe kultur* (Sept.-Oct. 1991): 24–31.

9. Uriel Weinreich, *Modern English-Yiddish, Yiddish-English Dictionary* (New York, 1968). The late author, himself a leading Yiddish scholar, was the son of Max Weinreich and the founder of the Yiddish Studies program at Columbia University.

10. Kats, 26.

11. Shekhter, 57. For a recent, post-ideological discussion of this issue in Yiddish literature, see Marc Miller, "The Artificiality of German in Modern Yiddish Poetry: A New Perspective on *Daytshmerish*," *Journal of Modern Jewish Studies* 4, no. 2 (July 2005): 123–35.

12. N. B. Minkov, "Hakdome," in *Pionern fun yidisher poeziye in amerike* (New York, 1956), 1:15.

13. See "A Language as Caliban," in *A Traveler Disguised* (New York, 1973), 34–66.

14. Uriel Weinreich, *College Yiddish* (New York: YIVO, 1999), 290–91. This book has appeared in many editions since its first publication in 1949.

5. The Jewish Representative

1. Heilman, 87.

Bibliography

Archival Sources

YIVO Institute for Jewish Research, New York.
Title: *Rosenfeld, Morris, 1862–1923: Papers, 1894–1962.* (5.4 linear feet)
Call Number: RG 431

Works by Morris Rosenfeld

Works in Yiddish

"Biz danen!" *Arbeter fraynd.* Sept. 14, 1888, 1.

Di blumenkete: A zamlung fun farshidene folks lider un poeziyen. New York: Folksadvokat, 1890.

Dos bukh fun libe. New York: M. Gurevitch, 1914.

Geklibene lider. Warsaw: Progress, 1905.

Gevelte shriftn. New York: Forward, 1912.

Gezamlte lider. New York: A. M. Evalenko, 1904.

Di gloke: Folks lider und revolutsiyonere gedikhte. New York: Gordon, 1888.

Grine tsores un andere shriftn. New York: Literatur, 1919.

Heinrich Heine: Daytshland's grester liriker. New York: International Library, 1906.

"In shap." *Di tsukunft,* Jan. 1893, 9.

Lider bukh: Ershter teyl. New York: Grover Brothers, 1897.

"Mayn yingele." *Di tsukunft.* Jan. 1893, 10.

Moris Rozenfelds briv. Edited by Yekhezkel Lifshitz. Buenos Aires: YIVO, 1955.

Poeziyen un lider. Ershter teyl: Natsiyonele lider. New York: A. H. Rosenberg, 1893.

"Di revolutsiyon." *Arbeter fraynd.* July 6, 1888, 1.

Shriftn fun Moris Rozenfeld. New York: A. M. Evalenko, 1908–10.

"Un alzo." *Arbeter fraynd.* Sept. 14, 1888, 1.

"Der veker der frayheyt." *Arbeter fraynd.* June 1, 1888, 1.

"Dos vign-lid." *Di nyu yorker yidishe folkstsaytung.* Jan. 14, 1887, 6.

"Vi lang nokh?" *Arbeter fraynd.* Sept. 14, 1888, 1.

Yehuda halevi: Der grester hebreyisher dikhter. New York: International Library, 1907.

"Dos yor 1886." *Di nyu yorker yidishe folkstsaytung,* Dec. 17, 1886, 5.

Works in Translation

CZECH

Zpevy z ghetta. Translated by Yaroslav Verkhlitski. Prague: n.p., 1903.

ENGLISH

Morris Rosenfeld: Selections from his Poetry and Prose. Translated by I. Goldberg and Max Rosenfeld. New York: YKUF, 1964.

Poems of Morris Rosenfeld. Translated by M. T. Cohen. New York: Retriever Books, 1979.

Songs from the Ghetto. Translated by Leo Wiener. Boston: Copeland and Day, 1898.

Songs from the Ghetto, 2nd ed. Translated by Leo Wiener. Boston: Small, Maynard, 1900.

Songs of Labor and Other Poems. Translated by Rose Pastor Stokes and Helena Frank. New York: Gorham Press, 1914.

The Teardrop Millionaire and Other Poems. Translated by New York: Manhattan Emma Lazarus Club, 1955.

GERMAN

Gedichte von Morris Rosenfeld. Translated by Friedrich Thiberger. Introduction by Friedlich Adler. Prague: Richard Brandeis, 1910.

Lieder des Ghetto. Translated by Berthold Feiwel. Berlin: H. Seemann Nachfolge, 1902.

HUNGARIAN

Költeményei. Translated by Arnold Kiss. Budapest: Deutsch Z. és Társa könyvkereskedese, 1908.

Költemények. Translated by Károly Csillag. Miskolc: Károly Csillag, 1925.

POLISH

Piesni pracy. Translated by Samuel Hirszhorn and Alfred Tom. Warsaw: n.p., 1906.

Wiazanka. Translated by Israel Waldman. Stanislav: Nakladem ksiegar E. Weidenfelda I Brata, 1903.

ROMANIAN

Cintece din ghetto. Translated by M. Rusu. Jasi: Iliescu, Grossu, 1904.

SERBIAN

Pjesme iz geta. Translated by Alexander Likht. Zagreb: n.p., 1906.

Anthologies and Almanacs Containing Rosenfeld Works

ENGLISH

Ausubel, N. and M. Ausubel, eds. *A Treasury of Jewish Poetry.* New York: Crown, 1957.

Betsky, Sarah Zweig, ed. and trans. *Onions and Cucumbers and Plums.* Detroit: Wayne State Univ. Press, 1981.

Harshav, Benjamin, and Barbara Harshav, eds. *American Yiddish Poetry.* Berkeley: Univ. of California Press, 1986.

Howe, Irving, and Eliezer Greenberg, eds. *A Treasury of Yiddish Poetry.* New York: Holt, Rinehart, and Winston, 1969.

Howe, Irving, Ruth R. Wisse, and Khone Shmeruk, eds. *The Penguin Book of Modern Yiddish Verse.* New York: Viking, 1987.

Imber, S. J., ed. *Modern Yiddish Poetry: An Anthology.* New York: East and West, 1927.

Raskin, P. M., ed. *Anthology of Modern Jewish Poetry.* New York: Behrman's, 1927.

Sinclair, Upton, ed. *The Cry for Justice: An Anthology of the Literature of Social Protest.* New York: Upton Sinclair, 1915.

Stedman, Edmund Clarence, ed. *American Anthology.* Cambridge, Mass., 1900.

Whitman, Ruth, ed. and trans. *An Anthology of Modern Yiddish Poetry.* Detroit: Wayne State Univ. Press, 1995.

FRENCH

Dobzynski, Charles, ed. *Le miroir d'un peuple: Anthologie de la poésie yiddish, 1870–1970.* Paris: Gallimard, 1970.

Fleg, Edmond, ed. *La vie juive dans la littérature.* Paris: Sulliver, 1951.

HEBREW

Halevi, A. Z., ed. *Mehashira hayidit be amerika.* Tel-Aviv: Hamenorah, 1967.

Meltzer, Shimshon, ed. *Al neharot.* Jerusalem: Mosad Bialik, 1956.

Niger, Sh., and Menakhem Ribalow, eds. *Akhisefer: Me'asef ledivrei sifrut min hashira hayidit.* New York: n.p., 1943.

Tirkel, Dov Ber, ed. *Shirei david.* Philadelphia: A. H. Rosenberg, 1904.

YIDDISH

Basin, M[oyshe], ed. *Amerikaner yidisher poeziye.* New York: n.p., 1940.

———, ed. *Finf hundert yor yidisher poeziye.* New York: Dos yidishe bukh, 1917.

Entin, Yoyl, ed. *Yidishe poetn: Hantbukh fun yidisher dikhtung.* Vol. 2. New York: Jewish National Workers' Alliance, 1927.

Fikhman, Y., ed. *Di yudishe muze.* Warsaw: Velt-bibliyotek, 1910.

Finkel, A., and S. Tomsini, eds. *Mut.* Moscow: Yidishe komunistishe bibliotek, 1920.

Kurland, Y. D., ed. *Di ershte yidishe arbeter dikhter.* Moscow: Tsenterfarlag, 1931.

Lande, Z., ed. *Di yidishe dikhtung in amerike biz yor 1919.* New York: Yidish, 1919.

Mayzl, N[akhman], ed. *Amerike in yidishn vort.* New York: YKUF, 1955.

Mlotek, K. and Y., eds. *Perl fun yidisher poeziye.* Tel-Aviv: Farlag Y. L. Peretz, 1974.

Rabinovitch, Y., ed. *Der arbeter in der yidisher literatur.* Moscow: Tsenterfar-lag, 1931.

Rozhansky, Shmuel, ed. *Moris Rozenfeld: oysgeklibene shriftn.* Buenos Aires: Yoysef Lifshitz-Fund, 1962.

All Other Sources

Abrams, M. H. *Natural Supernaturalism: Tradition and Revolution in Romantic Literature.* New York: Norton, 1971.

Allen, Jane. "College Settlement." *Encyclopedia of New York City,* ed. Kenneth T. Jackson, 254. New Haven: Yale Univ. Press, 1995.

Ayzland, Reuven. "Di naye vendung in der yidisher poeziye." In *Fun mentsh tsu mentsh,* edited by M.-L. Halpern, 32–36. New York: Farlag nyu york, 1915.

———. "Di yunge." *Shriftn* 1 (1912): 3–20.

Bal Dimyen (Nokhem Shtif). "Di yidishe poeziye: Ershter artikl: Moris Rozenfeld (der bal bekhi)." *Dos naye lebn* 3 (Mar. 1910): 33–47; 4 (Apr. 1910): 49–56.

Berkovich, Y. D., ed. *Dos Sholem Aleykhem bukh.* 2nd ed. New York: YIKUF, 1958.

Bialik, H. N. *Kol shirey Kh. N. Bialik.* Tel-Aviv: Dvir, 1966.

———. "Nokh a yorhundert," *Der yid* 16 (1899).

———. *Shirim.* Vol. 3. Edited by Dan Miron. Tel-Aviv: Dvir, 2000.

Bovshover, Yoysef. *Geklibene lider.* Edited by A. Agursky. Petrograd: Tsentraler yidisher komisariyat, 1918.

———. *Gezamlte shriftn.* New York: Fraye arbeter shtime, 1911.

———. *Lider.* Edited by Itsik Feffer. Kiev: Kultur-lige, 1930.

Brenner, Y. Kh. "Moris Rozenfeld." *Haktavim hayidim: di yidishe shriftn.* Jerusalem: Ben Gurion Univ. Press, 1985.

Braun, Sarah Alisa. Sarah Alisa Braun, "Translating the Ghetto: Leo Wiener, Morris Rosenfeld and the Invention of a Yiddish Poet." In "Becoming Authorities: Jews, Writing and the Dynamics of Literary Affiliation, 1890–1940," Ph.D. dissertation, University of Michigan, in progress.

Bronshteyn, Yashe. *Atake.* Moscow: Tsentraler Felker-Farlag fun F.S.S.R., 1930.

————. "Der stiln-kamf inem periyod fun militerishn komunism." *Prolit.* Nov.-Dec. 1929, 62–87; Feb. 1930, 26–77; Mar.-Apr. 1930, 108–22; May 1930, 66–82.

Brooks, Peter. *The Melodramatic Imagination.* New Haven: Yale Univ. Press, 1995.

Budianov, L. "A blondzhender poet." *Der nayer gayst* 1, no. 2 (Nov. 1897): 103–7.

Cahan, Ab[raham]. *Bleter fun mayn lebn.* New York, 1926–31.

————. "Moris Rozenfeld." *Forverts.* June 23, 1923, 3.

Dantses, M[ordkhe]. "A fertl yorhundert bagegenishn mit Moris Rozenfeld." *Der tog.* July 15, 1933, 5.

————. "Di troyerike letste yorn fun Moris Rozenfeld." *Der tog.* July 16, 1933.

Dobson, Joanne. "Reclaiming Sentimental Literature." *American Literature* 69, no. 2 (June 1997): 263–88.

Druyanow, Alter. *Ketavim Le-toldot hibbat zion ve-yishuv erets-yisrael.* Tel-Aviv: Hakibutz hameuhad, 1982.

Edelshtat, Dovid. *Edelshtats shriftn.* New York: Hebrew, 1923.

Engelman, J. "Erinerungen vegn farshtorbenem dikhter Moris Rozenfeld fun zaynem an amolikn shap-khaver." *Forverts.* June 19, 1929.

Entin, Yoyl. "Moris Rozenfeld: tsu zayn zekhtsik yorikn yovileyum." *Di tsukunft.* Feb. 1923, 130–31.

————. "A yidisher romantizm." In *Troymn un virklekhkeyt,* edited by Y. Adler and Y. Slonim, 14–24. New York, 1909.

Epstein, Melech. *Jewish Labor in the U.S.A.* Vol. 1. Hoboken, N.J.: Ktav, 1969.

Erik, Max. "Vegn dem tekst fun undzere proletarishe shrayber." *Shtern* (Minsk) 4–5 (Apr.-May 1931): 123–32.

Erlich, Victor. "Social and Aesthetic Criteria in Soviet Russian Criticism." In *Continuity and Change in Russian and Soviet Thought,* edited by Ernest J. Simmons, 398–416. Cambridge, Mass.: Harvard Univ. Press, 1955.

Fayn, Yitskhok. "Di yidishe velt (Louis Marshalls batsiyung tsu yidish)." In *Pinkes far der forshung fun der yidisher literatur un prese,* 3:334–44. New York: Congress for Jewish Culture, 1975.

Feffer, Itzik, and E. Finenberg, eds. *Vinchevsky, Morris; Dovid Edelshtat, Yoysef Bovshover. Geklibene lider.* Kiev: Kultur-Lige, 1931.

Fussell, Paul. *Poetic Meter and Poetic Form.* Rev. ed. New York: Random House, 1979.

Glatshteyn, Yankev. *Fun mayn gantser mi.* New York: Marstin Press, 1956.

———. "Moris Rozenfeld." In *Mit mayne fartogbikher,* 329–66. Tel-Aviv: Farlag Y. L. Peretz, 1963.

———. "Moris Rozenfeld der eseyist." In *Af greyte temes,* 54–57. Tel-Aviv: Farlag Y. L. Peretz, 1967.

———. "Moris Rozenfelds briv." In *In tokh genumen,* 1: 127–40. Buenos Aires: YIVO, 1960.

———. "Moris Rozenfelds geshtalt." *Di tsukunft.* Apr. 1962, 169–73.

Goldenthal, Edgar J. *Poet of the Ghetto.* Hoboken, N.J.: Ktav, 1998.

Goldenthal, Leon. *Toil and Triumph.* New York: Pageant, 1960.

Gordon, Mikhl. *Shirei M. Gordon: Yidishe lider fun Mikhl Gordon.* Warsaw: n.p., 1889.

Gordon, Y[ehuda] L[eyb]. *Kitvei Yehuda Leyb Gordon.* Tel-Aviv: Dvir, 1956.

Gotesfeld, Khone. "Di humoristishe zhurnaln: Der 'Kibitser' un "Groyser kundes.' " In *75 yor yidishe prese in amerike,* edited by Y. Glatshteyn, S. Niger, and H. Rogof, 97–99. New York: Yiddish Writers Union, 1945.

Hadda, Janet. "German and Yiddish in the Poetry of Jacob Glatstein." *Prooftexts* 1 (1981): 192–200.

Halpern, M[oyshe]-L[eyb]. "Der alter un der nayer Moris Rozenfeld." *Literatur un lebn* Mar. 1915: 100–12.

———. "An ofener brif tsu Moris Rozenfeld." *Der kibitzer.* Dec. 2, 1910.

———, ed. *Fun mentsh tsu mentsh.* New York: Farlag nyu york, 1915.

Halpern, M[oyshe]-L[eyb], and Menakhem Boreysho, eds. *Ist brodvey.* New York: Farlag fun mentsh tsu mentsh, 1916.

Hankin, Robert M. "Main Premises of the Communist Party in the Theory of Soviet Literary Controls." In *Continuity and Change in Russian and Soviet Thought,* edited by Ernest J. Simmons, 433–50. Cambridge, Mass.: Harvard Univ. Press, 1955.

Hapgood, Hutchins. *The Spirit of the Ghetto.* Cambridge, Mass.: Belknap Press, 1967.

Heilman, Robert Bechtold. *Tragedy and Melodrama: Versions of Experience.* Seattle: Univ. of Washington Press, 1968.

Heine, Heinrich. *Sämtliche Werke.* Vol. 1. Leipzig: Tempel, 1910.

Hollinger, David A. *In the American Province: Studies in the History and Historiography of Ideas.* Baltimore: Johns Hopkins Univ. Press, 1985.

Howe, Irving. *How We Lived: A Documentary History of Immigrant Jews in America, 1880–1930.* With Kenneth Libo. New York: R. Marek, 1979.

———. *World of Our Fathers.* With Kenneth Libo. New York: Simon and Schuster, 1976.

Hrushovski, Binyamin [Benjamin Harshav]. "On Free Rhythms in Modern Yiddish Poetry." In *The Field of Yiddish,* edited by Uriel Weinreich, 219–66. New York: Linguistic Circle of New York, 1954.

Ignatov, Dovid. "Sheyne grobyungeray un mise grobyungeray." *Shriftn* 1 (1912): 3–11.

———. "Di yugnt." *Di yugnt* 2 (Jan. 1908): 1–2.

Kats, Hirshe-Dovid. "A shtekele arayn, a shtekele aroys, di daytshmerishe gefar iz: Oys." *Yidishe kultur* Sep.-Oct.1991: 24–31.

Klingenstein, Susan. "A Philologist: The Adventures of Leo Wiener (1862–1939)." In *Jews in the American Academy, 1900–40: The Dynamics of Intellectual Assimilation,* 8–17. Syracuse: Syracuse Univ. Press, 1998.

Kobrin, Leon. "A blondzhender kritik (an entfer af Herr Budianovs artikl 'a blondzhender poet')." *Der nayer gayst* 1, no. 3 (Dec. 1897): 168–72.

Kurland, Dovid, ed. *Di ershte yidishe arbeter-dikhter (Moris Vinchevsky, Moris Rozenfeld, Dovid Edelshtat, Yoysef Bovshover).* Moscow: Tsentraler Felker-Farlag fun FSSR, Belorussian Section, 1931.

———. "Tsu der problem vegn di ershte yidishe proletarishe dikhter." *Afn visnshaftlekhn front* 5–6 (1934): 150–83.

———. "Vegn a nakhlesiker verk." *Afn visnshaftlekhn front* 3–4 (1933): 203–13.

Lande, Z[isho], ed. *Di yidishe dikhtung in amerike biz yor 1919.* New York: n.p., 1919.

Levitan, M. "Vegn Edelshtat's publisistik." *Visnshaft un revolutsiye* 3–4 (July-Dec. 1934): 147–59.

Leyeles, A. "M. Rozenfeld: 'Englisher poet.' " *Tog-Morgn Zhurnal.* June 10, 1962, 14.

———. "Refleksiyes." *In zikh.* July-Aug. 1923, 287–88.

Lifshitz, Yekhezkel. "Moris Rozenfeld un Leo Viner." *Fraye arbeter shtime*. July 15, 1962, 5.

——. "Di nyu yorker yidishe folkstsaytung." In *Pinkes far der forshung fun der yidisher literatur un prese*, edited by Khayim Bez, 3:251–318. New York: Congress for Jewish Culture, 1975.

Lifshutz, Ezekiel. "Morris Rosenfeld Attempts to Become an English Poet." *American Jewish Archives* 2, no. 22 (Nov. 1970): 121–37.

Liptzin, Sol. *The Flowering of Yiddish Literature*. New York: Thomas Yoseloff, 1963.

Litvakov, Moyshe. *Af tsvey frontn*. Moscow-Kharkov-Minsk: Tsentraler Felker-Farlag fun F.S.S.R., 1931.

——. *In umru*. Moscow: Shul un bukh, 1926.

——. "Yerushe un hegemoniye." *Der emes*. Feb. 14, 1926.

Madison, Charles. *Yiddish Literature: Its Scope and Major Writers*. New York: Frederick Ungar, 1968.

Marcosson, I. F. "A Voice from the Ghetto." *Bookman* 9, no. 1 (Mar. 1899): 68.

Marmor, K. "Bamerkungen er erineryngen tsu der gelegnhayt fun zayn ershtn yortsayt." *Frayheyt*. June 24, 1924.

——. "Der foter fun der yidishe poeziye in amerike." *Yidishe kultur* July 1948: 5–8.

——. "Di froy fun a yidishn shrayber / shtrikhn un gedankn vegn der ersht farshtorbener almone fun dem dikhter Moris Rozenfeld." *Frayheyt*. July 17–18, 1927.

——. "Fun Moris Rozenfelds literarishe yerushe." In *Pinkes*, 200–12. New York: YIVO, 1927–28.

——. "Moris Rozenfelds satirishe lider kegn der geler prese in amerike." *Visnshaft un revolutsiye* Jan.-Mar. 1935: 3–9.

——. "Der onheyb fun a yidisher literatur in amerike." In *Almanakh fun internatsiyonaln arbeter ordn*, 335–64. New York: Jewish National Workers' Alliance, 1940.

Mayzl, Nakhman. "Der dikhter mit tife vidershprukhn," *Yidishe kultur* July 1948, 8–10.

——. "Moris Rozenfeld." In *Noente un vayte*, 32–40. Vilna: B. Kletskin, 1926.

——. "Moris Rozenfeld in likht fun der yidisher kritik (tsu zayn 100stn geburtstog)." In *YKUF almanakh 1967*, 60–80. New York: Grenich, 1967.

———, ed. *Tsum hundertstn geburtstog fun Moris Rozenfeld*. New York: YKUF, 1962.

Merison, Y[ankev] M. "Tsu Moris Rozenfeld's onheyb." In *Pinkes*, 269. New York: YIVO, 1927–28.

Milkh, Yankev. " 'Printsipiyele' kritik: an antvort af L. Kobrin's 'blondzhende kritik.' " *Di naye tsayt* 1, no. 4 (Jan. 1898): 242–46; no. 5 (Feb. 1898): 292–97.

Miller, Marc. "The Artificiality of German in Modern Yiddish Poetry: A New Perspective on *Daytshmerish*." *Journal of Modern Jewish Studies* 4, no. 2 (July 2005): 123–35.

———. "Modernism and Persona in the Works of Moyshe-Leyb Halpern," *Yiddish* 11, no. 1 (1998): 48–71.

———. "Morris Rosenfeld." In *Dictionary of Literary Biography: Yiddish Writers*. Columbia, S.C.: Bruccoli, Clark, Layman, forthcoming.

———. "Tradition and Hegemony: Soviet Yiddish Literary Critics and American Sweatshop Poetry in the Interwar Period." *East European Jewish Affairs* 35, no. 2 (Dec. 2005): 189–207.

Minkov, N[okhem] B[orekh]. "Moris Rozenfeld." In *Yidishe klasiker poetn*, 67–98. New York: n.p., 1937.

———. *Pionern fun der yidisher poeziye in amerike*. New York: Grenich, 1956.

Miron, Dan. "Folklore and Antifolklore in the Yiddish Fiction of the Haskala." In *The Image of the Shtetl and Other Studies of Modern Jewish Literary Imagination*, 49–80. Syracuse: Syracuse Univ. Press, 2000.

———. "H. N. Bialik and the Prophetic Mode in Modern Hebrew Poetry." In *The B. G. Rudolph Lectures in Judaic Studies, New Series, Lecture Two*. Syracuse: Syracuse Univ. Press, 2000.

———. *A Traveler Disguised*. New York: Schocken Books, 1973.

Nelson, Cary. *Repression and Recovery*. Madison: Univ. of Wisconsin Press, 1989.

Niger, Sh. "Mer altheymish vi amerikanish." *Di tsukunft*. Apr. 1940, 212–17.

———. "Moris Rozenfeld (tsu zayn 50-yorikn yubiley)." *Di yidishe velt* 5 (May 1913): 85–98.

————. "Onheyb fun der proletarisher-yidisher literatur." *Di tsukunft.* Sept. 1940, 529–33.

Olgin, M. "Moris Rozenfeld." In *In der velt fun gezangn,* 129–42. New York, 1919.

————. "Moris Rozenfeld." In *Kultur un folk,* 191–201. New York: YKUF, 1949.

Payne, William Morton. "Rosenfeld's *Songs from the Ghetto.*" *Dial.* Jan. 16, 1899, 54.

Peltz, Rakhmiel. "The Dehebraization Controversy in Soviet Yiddish Language Planning: Standard or Symbol?" In Joshua Fishman, ed., *Readings in the Sociology of Jewish Languages,* 125–50. Leiden: E. J. Brill, 1985.

————. "The Undoing of Language Planning from the Vantage of Cultural History: Two Twentieth Century Yiddish Examples." In *Undoing and Redoing Corpus Planning,* edited by M. Clyne, 327–56. Berlin: Mouton de Gruyter, 1997.

Pinès, M[eyer Isser]. *Die Geschichte der jüdischdeutschen Literatur.* Translated by Georg Hecht. Leipzig: G. Engel, 1913.

————. *Di geshikhte fun der yidisher literatur.* Edited by Bal Makhshoves. Warsaw: B. Shimin, 1911.

————. "Histoire de la littérature judéo-allemande." Ph.D. dissertation, Univ. of Paris, 1910.

Pomerants, Alexander. "Politishe kritik." In *Di sovetishe harugey malokhes,* 302–30. Buenos Aires: YIVO, 1962.

Portnoy, Edward. "The Creation of a Jewish Cartoon Space in the Yiddish Presses of New York and Warsaw, 1889–1939." Ph.D. dissertation, Jewish Theological Seminary of America, 2006.

Prilutski, Noyekh. "Metodologishe bamerkungen tsum problem datshmerish." *Yidish far ale* 8 (Oct. 1938): 201–9.

Reyzn, Zalman, ed. *Leksikon fun der yiddisher literatur, prese, un philologiye.* Vilna: Vilner farlag, 1916.

————, ed. *Leksikon fun der yiddisher literatur.* Vilna: Vilner farlag, 1928.

Rivkin, Borukh. *Grunt tendensn fun der yidisher literatur in amerike.* New York: YKUF, 1948.

————. "Moris Rozenfeld: Der ershter aroystsubafrayen zayn lid fun unter der takhlis distsiplin." In *Yidishe dikhter in amerike,* by Borukh Rivkin, 1:35–48. New York: CYCO, 1947.

Rogoff, Hillel. "Beletristn, mitglider fun der redaksiye: Kobrin, Libin un Moris Rozenfeld." In *Der gayst fun Forverts,* 61–72. New York: Forward, 1954.

Royznblit, H. "Stires in dem tragishn lebn fun Moris Rozenfeld." *Di tsukunft.* Jan. 1959, 21–25.

Shatsky, Y, "Moris Rozenfeld in likht fun zayne briv," *Zamlbikher* 1 (1936): 339–66.

Shaykovsky, Z. *Katalog fun der YIVO oyshtelung: Moris Rozenfeld un zayn tsayt.* New York: YIVO, 1962.

Shekhter, Mordkhe. "Fun dizn-dazn tsun a yidish yidish." In *Laytish mame-loshn,* 1:53–121. New York: Yidish-lige, 1986.

Shlossman, Mort. "Memories of Morris Rosenfeld." *Jewish News* (Newark, N.J.). June 29, 1962, 20.

Shmeruk, Khone. *Pirsumim yehudiim bevrit hamoatsot 1917–60.* Jerusalem: Historical Society of Israel, 1961.

———."Yiddish Literature in the U.S.S.R." In *The Jews in Soviet Russia since 1917,* edited by Lionel Kochan, 232–68. Oxford: Oxford Univ. Press, 1978.

Shtarkman, Moyshe. "Di anshteyung fun der yidishe prese in amerike." In *Zamlbukh tsu der geshikhte fun der yidishe prese in amerike,* edited by Yankev Shatsky, 13–21. New York: Yidisher kultur gezelshaft, 1934.

———. "Moris Rozenfeld's onheyb." In *Pinkes,* 53–57. New York: YIVO, 1927–28.

Simmons, Ernest J. "Review." In *Continuity and Change in Russian and Soviet Thought,* edited Ernest J. Simmons, 451–69. Cambridge, Mass.: Harvard Univ. Press, 1955.

Slonim, Yoyl. "Der tragisher sof fun a groysn dikhter." *Der tog.* June 26, 1923.

Sobel, Yakov Tsvi. *Shir zahav likhvod yisrael hazaken/Yisrol der alte.* New York: n.p., 1877.

Stanislawski, Michael. *For Whom Do I Toil: Jeudah Leib Gordon and the Crisis of Russian Jewry.* New York: Oxford Univ. Press, 1988.

———. "Vom Jugendstil zum 'Judendstil': Universalismus und Nationalismus im Werk Ephraim Moses Liliens." In *Zionistische Utopie: Is-raelische Realität*, edited by Michael Brenner and Yfaat Weiss, 87–95. Munich: C. H. Beck, 1999.

Szajkowski, Z. *Morris Rosenfeld and His Time.* New York: YIVO, 1962.

Tabachnik, Avrom. *Dikhter un dikhtung.* New York: Knight, 1965.

———. "Moris Rozenfeld: 20 yor nokh zayn toyt." In *Literarishe zamlungen*, edited by M. Ghitzis and Mates Deitsh, 9–39. Chicago: n.p., 1943.

Timasheff, Nicholas. *The Great Retreat: The Growth and Decline of Communism in Russia.* New York: Dutton, 1946.

Tschernikhovsky, Shaul. *Poemot ve-ideliyot.* Vol. 2. Tel-Aviv: Am Oved, 1990.

Vevyorke, Avrom. "Arop mitn kleynbirglekhn kheyrem." *Der emes*, Apr. 10, 1927.

———. *In shturm.* Kharkov: Melukhisher Natsmindfarlag, 1932.

———. "Reviziye." *Prolit.* May 1928, 27–36.

———. *Reviziye.* Kharkov: Melukhe-Farlag Literatur un Kunst, 1931.

———. "Undzer yikhes," *Shtern* 4 (Apr. 1930): 80–90; 5–6 (May-June 1930): 132–39; 7–8 (July-Aug. 1930): 76–80.

Vinchevsky, Morris. *Gezamlte verk.* Vol. 2. New York: Frayheyt, 1927.

———. *Lider un gedikhte.* New York: Frayheyt, 1910.

Viner, Meyer. *Tsu der geshikhte fun der yidisher literatur in 19tn yorhundert*, 170–71. New York: YKUF, 1946.

———. "Tsu der problem fun literarisher yerushe." *Shtern* 4–5 (Apr.-May 1932): 120–43.

Viner, Meyer, and A. Gurshteyn, eds. *Problemes fun kritik.* Moscow: Emes, 1933.

Vital, David. *The Origins of Zionism.* Oxford: Clarendon Press, 1975.

Werses, Shmuel. "Hedei hasatira shel lukianus be-sifrut ha-haskala ha-ivrit." In *Megamot ve tsurot be-sifrut ha-haskalah*, 223–48. Jerusalem: Magnes Press.

Weinreich, Max. "Daytshmerish toyg nit." *Yidish far ale* 4(June 1938): 101.

Weinreich, Uriel. *College Yiddish.* New York: YIVO, 1999.

———. "On the Cultural History of Yiddish Rime." In *Essays on Jewish Life and Thought*, edited by Joseph L. Blau, 423–42. New York: Columbia Univ. Press, 1959.

Wiener, Leo. *The History of Yiddish Literature in the Nineteenth Century.* New York: Scribner's, 1899.

Wisse, Ruth R. *A Little Love in Big Manhattan.* Cambridge, Mass.: Harvard Univ. Press, 1988.

———. "Di Yunge: Immigrants or Exiles?" *Prooftexts* 1, no. 1 (Jan. 1981): 43–61.

———. "Di Yunge and the Problem of Jewish Aestheticism." *Jewish Social Studies* 38 (Summer-Fall 1976): 265–76.

———. *What Shall Live and What Shall Die: The Makings of a Yiddish Anthology.* Cincinnati: Univ. of Cincinnati, Judaic Studies Program, 1989.

Yeshurun, Y. *Moris Rozenfeld bibliographiye.* Buenos Aires: YIVO, 1962.

Zhirmunskii, V. *Introduction to Metrics: The Theory of Verse.* Translated by C. F. Brown. London: Mouton, 1966.

Zunser, Elyokim. *Tsvantsik yidishe folks-lider.* New York: n.p., 1898.

Index

Abramovitch, S. Y. (Mendele
Moykher-Sforim), 14, 17, 21, 33,
47, 50, 53, 54, 58, 144
Abrams, M. H., 66
Adler, Felix, 19
"Afn buzm fun yam" (On the Bosom
of the Ocean) (Rosenfeld), 22, 37
"Afn toytn-gortn" (In the Garden of
the Dead) (Rosenfeld), 111–13
Agursky, A., 51
Aleykhem, Sholem, ix, 10, 17, 21, 25,
33, 35, 47, 50, 53, 54, 58, 144
"Alte sisteme, Di" (The Old System)
(Rosenfeld), 7
"Ambelens" (Ambulance)
(Rosenfeld), 74–75
"Ambulance." *See* "Ambelens"
American Anthology (Stedman), 18
American Yiddish newspapers, 3
American Yiddish Poetry, 61
American Yiddish Poetry Anthology, 59,
169n. 77
American Yiddish press, ix, xi, 3, 13,
21, 22, 25, 30, 49, 70, 72, 74, 149
Amerikaner (American), 28
"Among the Dead." *See* "Tsvishn di
toyte"
Anarchism, ix, 146

Arbeter fraynd (Worker's Friend), 7, 10
Arbeter tsaytung, Der (The Worker's
Newspaper), ix, 4, 10
"Arbeter un frayhayts-lider" (Worker
and Freedom Poems), 23
Asch, Sholem, ix, 41
Ashmeday, Der (Asmodeus), 21
Asmodeus. *See Ashmeday, Der*
"At the Shop and at Home." *See* "In
shap un der heym"
"Awake My People." *See* "Hakitsah
ami"
Ayzland, Reuven, 41, 44

"Baby in the Forest, The." *See* "Ufele
in vald, Dos"
Badkhones, 53, 168n. 60
"Bam breg vaser" (By the Waterside)
(Rosenfeld), 49
"Barukh me-magenza" (Barukh of
Mayence) (Tschernikhovsky),
117
"Barukh of Mayence." *See* "Barukh
me-magenza"
Basin, Moyshe, 59–60
Baytsh, Der (The Whip), 26
Bell, The. See Gloke, Di

189

Other titles in Judaic Traditions in Literature, Music, and Art

American Artists, Jewish Images
Matthew Baigell

The Dybbuk and the Yiddish Imagination: A Haunted Reader
Joachim Neugroschel, trans. & ed.

A House with Seven Windows: Short Stories
Kadya Molodowsky; Leah Schoolnik, trans.

The Image of the Shtetl and Other Studies of Modern Jewish Literary Imagination
Dan Miron

In Harness: Yiddish Writers' Romance with Communism
Gennady J. Estraikh

In Lieu of Memory: Contemporary Jewish Writing in France
Thomas Nolden

Intimations of Difference: Dvora Baron in the Modern Hebrew Renaissance
Sheila E. Jelen

Nathan and His Wives: A Novel
Miron C. Izakson; Ken Frieden, ed.; Betsy Rosenberg, trans.

What Must Be Forgotten: The Survival of Yiddish Writing in Zionist Palestine
Yael Chaver

The Wishing Ring: A Novel
S. Y. Abramovitsh; Michael Wex, trans.